Two hundred years
of London Justice

The story of Hampstead
and Clerkenwell Magistrates' Courts

Gillian Tindall

*With warmest
good wishes &
thanks for
your help*

Gillian

23/10/01

Camden History Society
© Gillian Tindall 2001

ISBN 0-904491-52-8

Edited by   F Peter Woodford

Designed by   Ivor Kamlish

Indexed by   David A Hayes

Contents

I am grateful to several former members of the West Central Division - Regina Lewis, Myrna Whiteson, Anita Morgan, Jeffrey Aubrey and Sydney Jacques, and other colleagues including Jeffrey Bryer of the Inner London Magistrates Service and Rodney Wasserson, Clerk to the East Central Division. Dr Stephen Porter of the Survey of London has answered some historical questions and Professor Derek Keene of the Institute of Historical Research, London University, has been generous with his time, interest and suggestions. John Richardson and Christopher Wade of the Camden History Society have been unfailingly helpful: indeed I am most grateful to the Council of CHS in general for making it possible for me to write this book, and especially to my editor Dr Peter Woodford for the time and trouble he has taken.

My especial thanks also to those who have read the finished typescript for me and made useful suggestions: to His Honour Michael McMullan, some time of Wood Green Crown Court; and to Malcolm Holmes, Borough Archivist of Camden, on whose expertise in the history of local administration I have much relied. Most of all, I owe a debt of gratitude to Michael Pascoe, former Chief Clerk to the Justices of the West Central Division, who read the typescript but who also was responsible on his own initiative for salvaging a few invaluable pictures and documents, and who supplied me with information on the unique administration of Hampstead Court.

My thanks too to the staff of the Magistrates' Association and their library, where I spent a number of pleasant and rewarding hours; thanks too, as ever, to the staffs of the British Library and the London Library, and also to the staff of the Guildhall Library. And particular thanks to the Head Archivist and staff of the London Metropolitan Archives, where the court registers and minute books finally come to rest, and whose new building is, by a happy chance, situated in the heart of Clerkenwell. I am particularly grateful to those who located Hampstead's oldest surviving minute book for me in an unexpected place, and for permission to reproduce a page from it. My thanks also to the Revd Stephen Tucker of Hampstead Parish Church.

At times I have felt, too, a surge of warmth towards those dead and gone magistrates, particularly the lay ones whose years of effort brought no financial reward, and who did their best often in circumstances very different from our own. I can only hope that, if they could read this book, they would on the whole feel gratified, even surprised, to find their names preserved and all their labours not utterly forgotten.

The terms in common use about courts can be confusing. For clarity's sake, I have often used 'courthouse' to apply to to the building and 'courtroom' to the room where the hearings take place, although just 'court' is commonly used in speech for both of these. 'The court' can also be used in a more abstract sense, as in 'The Court finds you guilty', in which case it applies to the person or persons presiding over the proceedings. This person or persons are also known as 'the Bench', although the same term is used to indicate the entire body of magistrates who are allocated to that Division.

The designation 'Chairman' (never chairwoman or chairperson) is applied to the person who is agreed by the Bench to be its head. In the past, this would normally have been the man of most senior rank socially, or sometimes the most senior in age and experience; today, it will be a man or woman formally elected by the whole Bench, but always someone of experience and ability. In the past, too, when Benches only sat once or twice a week, the chairman of the Bench was more often present than not and would automatically take the Chair in court – i.e. the central position as spokesman in charge of the court in a sitting Bench of three people. Today, when large numbers of magistrates are rotated to sit turn by turn, the Chair in court is taken by any member of that day's Bench who has done extra training, and is therefore qualified as 'a presiding justice'.

A Clerk to the court, whether a senior Clerk in charge of a whole Division or one of his juniors, is an important and highly qualified person, which is why I spell 'Clerk' throughout with a capital C. In fact, from 2000, Clerks have been given the additional title of 'Legal advisors to the Justices', but I refer to them here in the way they always have been known. Similarly, Stipendiary Magistrates are now known as 'District Judges', but they figure in this history under their historical name.

This book contains an occasional reference to courts higher than the magistrates' courts – the one-time Quarter Sessions and Assize Courts, conflated in 1971 into Crown Courts. Some magistrates' court cases have always been sent to these higher courts for trial by jury; in the past, magistrates used to sit in Quarter Sessions, with various degrees of responsibility, and today they still sit with judges on appeals in Crown Court. I have avoided, however, going into the changing fortunes of these courts since I do not want to complicate the account. Within the London area, JPs have played a less important role in Quarter Sessions in the last 150 years than their provincial colleagues have. During that same period, more and more types of case have become triable in the Petty Sessions Courts – that is to say, before magistrates alone.

This is essentially a book about two magistrates' courts, though I hope these two classic examples may stand for many others. I hope too that their history will provide diversion and interest for readers who do not personally know either Hampstead or Clerkenwell, or indeed London itself, but will enjoy exploring the world our ancestors knew from an unusual viewpoint.

A note on currency

A pre-decimal pound comprised 20 shillings;
    12 pence made a shilling (now 5p).
8*d* stood for eightpence ($3^{1}/_{2}$p);
3*s* or 3/- for three shillings (15p);
1/6 for one shilling and sixpence ($7^{1}/_{2}$p);
£16.15.4 for sixteen pounds, fifteen shillings
    and fourpence (about £16.77)
and these abbreviations have been used in the text
    and in the quotations where appropriate.

1 The end of the story

In the summer of 1998 the Chief Clerk to the Justices, who had
for the past 19 years been responsible for the West Central Division
of the Inner London magistrates' courts, went with one of his lay
magistrates on a visit to Hampstead courthouse. There had been a
Bench of local magistrates in Hampstead since the Middle Ages; its
court had sat variously in private houses, in the committee room of
the workhouse, or (since the mid-Victorian era) in accommodation
above the then police station in the High Street. But since 1913 the
magistrates had been sitting regularly in the substantial red-brick,
purpose-built courthouse on the corner of Rosslyn Hill and
Downshire Hill. Five or six days out of seven, week in week out
with no holiday breaks, year in year out, the court had gone about
its work there as a part of the vast machinery on which society runs.
Like every court in the land, it had been imbued with traditional
forms and practices, yet it changed with the times because it had
been in itself an expression of those times and of changing values
and concepts.

'Had been' – because the courthouse was now shut. The Chief
Clerk and the magistrate were visiting it to retrieve a few items
that had been presented to the Bench in the past: an oil painting
or two that hung in the Justices' retiring room, a photograph of the
members of the Bench in 1924, an engraved silver inkstand. How
solid and permanent the resting place of these objects must have
seemed to the donors! People grow old and are replaced, buildings
come and go, but the local Bench was the Bench and would go on,
as it had done for centuries. But no more. Hampstead courthouse
had been, in recent years, almost the last in London to have only
one courtroom. The Clerkenwell court down near King's Cross, with
which it had been paired to form the West Central Division since
1965, had only two. In the interests of rationalisation, streamlining,
saving money, modern security, reorganisation and similarly
optimistic or opportunistic government goals, the Hampstead court
had recently been shut down. Clerkenwell was to follow suit a few
months later, at the end of 1998. The Bench was disbanded, its
members dispersed, along with its workload, to other, more distant
courts at Highbury, Westminster or Tower Bridge. And so a very long
era in the history of local justice came, almost silently, to an end.

The silence, in fact, was what struck the Clerk and the magistrate most. The doors had been carefully locked, with alarms set; even the heating was still inappropriately on. The courtroom itself, with its raised Bench and royal coat of arms, its light oak panelling, iron-railed dock and notices about witnesses leaving the place when their cases were called, was exactly as it had always been, a theatre waiting for the usual play to begin. It seemed that at any moment there would be footsteps in the backstage corridors, voices in the hall, heralding the daily performance. Then on would bustle a large and varied cast of court staff, magistrates, solicitors, probation officers, police, security, ushers and witnesses – and the endless procession in and out of the dock of the defendants, loquacious or mute, conciliatory or defiant, for whom the whole show was being run. The formal, staged nature of a courtroom hearing fulfils an important function: justice is in this way seen to be done. Both prosecution and defence have clear roles, and no case can be concluded till each has played its allotted part.

But this theatre had 'gone dark'. Even though the elaborate skylight that is traditional in court rooms still poured its daily light down into the windowless space, nothing stirred in its illumination and no one saw it. Apparently, the solid people who had so long populated it had now melted like Shakespeare's actors into thin air. The whole impression of power, continuity and permanence which a court creates had, after all, been an insubstantial pageant, leaving not a wrack behind – not even a drift of legal papers.

Magistrates and court staff, for all their air of being in charge of the place, *are* only actors, passing through; they have no stake of ownership in the place, nor do they own its past, however closely they have been concerned in it. The huge amount of potential archive material that any court's daily work generates does not remain there long. It does not belong to the Bench, but to the Lord Chancellor's Department or the Home Office or the police or the Probation Service or to innumerable separate solicitors' offices. Much of it is either confidential or ephemeral; in either case it will be thrown away after half a dozen years, if not much sooner. Unlike, say, proceedings of local authorities or public companies, what goes on in courts by way of discussion and decision-taking is not preserved in the public domain. It is the live, day-to-day court hearings that constitute open and public justice. As for this day-to-day running of a court – its procedures, its customs, the interchanges it has seen, its individual relationships, its collective preoccupations – little is ever recorded in any permanent or retrievable way.

Eventually the London court registers, which are the telegraphically brief official record of cases and their outcomes, come to rest in what is now the London Metropolitan Archives. With any luck, most of the magistrates' 'minute' books, which are not minutes of discussion but simply scrawled details of evidence that give a fuller impression of contested cases, join them there. After a lapse of 30 years, researchers are allowed to consult them, though inevitably by then many of the personal memories that might help to flesh out the bare bones of fact are no longer available.

One curious result of this lack of permanent or coherent documentation of anything but the outcome of cases is that magistrates' courts have been largely ignored by general social historians. Again and again one finds studies in which the doings of the local authorities of different eras are given adequate weight but in which the topic of local justice is passed over almost in silence. Even magistrates' courts in themselves – large buildings by their nature, and some of them now listed as being of architectural interest (as is Clerkenwell Court) – tend to go unmentioned, while Town Halls, inns and sites of ancient gibbets all get a share of attention, and schools get a section all to themselves. Very occasionally, local newspaper reports of long-ago trials are quoted, but this is almost always because the case concerned is sensational or piquant in its own right, rather than because it is a genuine marker for the social evolution and change to which the courts bear constant witness.

At least in recent decades registers and minute books have been conserved in a fairly ordered way. It was not always so. In many instances in the past, the mere pulling down and rebuilding or relocation of a courthouse led to the wholesale destruction of any records it was harbouring. A classic early example of this occurred in 1881, when the original house at Bow Street was swept away and with it a unique archive concerning the first magistrates' courthouse in the United Kingdom. The rebuilding of Clerkenwell courthouse 1904-6 was presumably accompanied by a similarly brisk disregard for history, since the earliest surviving registers date from 1905, although as a court in the essential sense it is one of the oldest in London.

Hampstead, perhaps because of its different composition and history (of which more below) has fared better. A continuous run of Hampstead minutes books starts in 1867, and one survives from much earlier in that century. Probably the records lay for a long time undisturbed in the houses of individual magistrates, and these men turned out to be better custodians than any formal system. This, perhaps, already tells us something about that idiosyncratic London Bench whose roots lay so firmly in its rural origins.

2 Town and country justice

Hampstead is one of those old Middlesex villages whose rural identity goes back more than 1000 years but which, at different rates over the last three centuries, have been gradually absorbed into the ever-growing city near at hand. Islington, Highgate and Kentish Town have all shared this fate in their time. But while most of these districts disappeared into London so completely that any sense of countryside departed from them, Hampstead retained its rural air well into the 20th century, and attracted the kind of affluent, cultured and influential families who, in turn, made sure that the cruder aspects of urbanisation were kept at bay.

This was in a large part due to its prime situation on a hill too steep to be traversed by any major route to the north, but also to the extent and renown of Hampstead Heath. Already, by the late 18th century, significant numbers of well-to-do families were settled in Hampstead. Poets celebrated it, Constable painted it. This in turn ensured that 19th-century development pressures threatening the Heath and its surrounding farmlands were vigorously resisted. Families such as the Hoares, who lived in Heath House and other nearby substantial properties, and the Bosanquets, who lived at 'The Firs' near the Spaniards Inn, defended their territory and made sure that Hampstead's aspect of gentlemanly rurality was retained and even enhanced. It was these same families and their kind who continued through successive generations to provide Justices for the Hampstead Bench in the best traditions of the rural landowning classes. (Justices of the Peace, often known as JPs, and lay magistrates are one and the same thing).

Of course, these Hampstead people were not really country gentry. The Hoares were a Quaker banking family whose wealth lay down the hill in the City, as did that of the Bosanquets. Other 19th-century magistrates included doctors, retired military men, company presidents, a successful civil engineer, and citizens simply taking their ease as 'gentlemen of independent means' on the proceeds of Britain's industrial supremacy. But they were educated and energetic, well able to play the role of country squire and eager to do so. They form collectively an example of a particularly British phenomenon, the conviction that a rural lifestyle is morally and socially superior to an urban one. Between them, they assured the continuation of the sort of local administration in Hampstead for which the Justice of the Peace system had been created in the Middle Ages.

In the rest of London, the system had been breaking down ever since the 17th century, as society became more fragmented, and upper and lower classes no longer lived cheek by jowl in crowded city streets. Londoners of wealth and ability, who had in any case often moved into more spacious and airy houses in newer districts, were no longer interested in administering the daily affairs and arbitrating in the squabbles of older, poorer London districts. Instead, the job was left to petty tradesmen, artisans, tavern keepers and the like, with little education or tradition of public service. Naturally, corruption followed: as early as 1601 there were complaints in Parliament about 'basket Justices' who allegedly carried baskets to receive gifts from those who appeared before them. By the turn of the 18th century the existence of these 'trading Justices', as they were also known, was an established scandal. 'Needy, mean, ignorant and rapacious' magistrates pocketed bail money, exacted protection money and invented other devices for enriching themselves both from accused and accusers, so that their decisions came to be driven by this motive rather than by a desire to keep the peace and dispense justice. The reputation of these Middlesex and Westminster Justices eventually became so bad that even respectable tradesmen avoided the job, and Edmund Burke could declare furiously after the Gordon Riots in 1780 that the Benches were composed of 'the scum of the earth – carpenters, brickmakers and shoe makers; some of whom were notoriously men of such infamous character that they were unworthy of any employ whatever, and others so ignorant that they could scarcely write their own names.'

It was against this background that the enigmatic Justice Thomas de Veil had already, in the mid-18th century, constituted himself a one-man detective force to bring a little awe and fear to miscreants in the London streets. Both his crusading role and his Bow Street house in which he established his court were later taken on by the Fielding brothers – Henry, the novelist, and John his blind half-brother. They founded the first office recognisable as something like a modern magistrates' court, with their own police force (the Bow Street runners) and their own reputation for probity and public service. Near the end of the century, Bow Street became the model for the first seven 'public offices' set up in the London area which subsequently became known as 'police courts'.

Each court was assigned six constables to help keep law and order. Three 'fit and able magistrates' were paid to attend turn by turn in this set location at fixed hours six days out of seven, for which each was paid a respectable salary of £400 a year. In this way the first *stipendiary* magistrates appeared, very different beings from the old 'trading Justices' sitting at whim in rooms over public houses. To begin with, these full-time paid magistrates were not lawyers, but in the early decades of the 19th century it became first customary for them to have legal qualifications and then obligatory. By then, their £400 per annum had been doubled and they were precluded from taking on any other legal commitments.

Thus London acquired two distinct types of magistrate, the JPs and the stipendiaries working in parallel, each with their own court hearings. In practice, as the 19th century went by and the type of work required of magistrates altered for different reasons, the stipendiaries took over more and more of it, and most of the Middlesex Justices were reduced to little more than licensing the sale of liquor. But of course this applied only in areas where a police office was established.

The first seven offices set up in 1792 were in the parishes of Clerkenwell, St Margaret's Westminster, St James's Westminster, Shoreditch, Whitechapel, Shadwell and Southwark. (The City proper had its own magistrates, sitting in the Guildhall, where they remain to this day.) At first the Clerkenwell office was in Hatton Garden, within the parish of St Andrew Holborn, in one of those enclaves known as 'Liberties' which made a chequerboard of the London administrative map until the coming of the metropolitan boroughs. But its *district* was Clerkenwell, and in or about 1841 it was transferred further north to a new building on a site in Bagnigge Wells Road, renamed King's Cross Road in 1863. The oldest part of the recently closed Clerkenwell Magistrates' court, the low two-storey building on the southern side, is a part of the original complex. So, for the next century and a quarter, Clerkenwell pursued its urban destiny as a full-time stipendiary court untroubled by JPs.

In the great reorganisation of 1965 which, after more than 150 years, united the two types of London magistrate into a single system, Clerkenwell and Hampstead Courts were joined together to become the West Central Division of the Inner London Magistrates'

Courts Service. It was, on the face of it, an odd coupling.
Clerkenwell was an old-style police court always presided over by
stipendiaries, and it continued to be served by them for the next 20
years, with lay Justices making only occasional descents there from
the gentler world of Hampstead to fill in for a stipendiary taking the
day off. But the Hampstead Justices were unlike those in the rest of
London, who had been marginalised for generations by the
supremacy of the stipendiaries. They were entirely accustomed to
sitting on a wide range of cases because the Hampstead court had
remained over generations an entirely lay Bench – a country-style
Petty Sessional Division in its own right.

In 1840, when the public offices were becoming formalised into
police courts, it had been decided that Hampstead was too thinly
populated and too law-abiding to be allocated a 'resident
magistrate'. Subsequently, even though Hampstead and most of the
slopes leading up to it were becoming built up, the Hoares and the
Bosanquets and their dynastic successors continued to maintain
their hold on local justice. They actually spread their rule further,
over the new district of Belsize Park and down to the humbler
streets of Kentish Town.

The accelerating growth of London in the last three decades of
the 19th century meant, in most districts, that a rising commercial
lower middle class tended to take over the reins of local power. But
in Hampstead, exceptionally, a large proportion of those who moved
into the newer houses were moneyed and influential people of much
the same class as the older gentry, so that the same traditions
continued. After 1888, in the whole of what had now become the
London County Council area, Hampstead Bench alone managed to
retain its historic right of full jurisdiction and its autonomous
constitution. Only in very recent times, from the late 1980s, did a
stipendiary ever sit there, and even that was only on one day a week;
on that day, Hampstead Justices regularly sat in his court in
Clerkenwell.

'Hampstead was always an anomaly', Chief Clerk Michael
Pascoe remembers. 'It was the court that time forgot. When I was
first there as a junior Clerk in 1967 even the book-keeping was unlike
any other court. The London courts were audited by the receiver of
the Metropolitan Police District, but I seem to remember that we
were directly under the Lord Chancellor's office. It had a different
starting time too: 10 am, when all the other courts were 10:30. But

it was also the only court where magistrates could sit half-days.'

The true anomaly of Hampstead was brought home to me when I was combing through such year-lists of Justices as have survived and come to rest at London Metropolitan Archives – by no means a complete set. For much of the 19th century Hampstead Justices figured in the general list of Middlesex Justices, though once Justices began (after 1868) to be listed under Metropolitan Divisions also, no Division appears for Hampstead – correctly, but illogically. Then for a couple of years in the 1890s, two neat little blue books appear, each labelled 'County of London, Lists of Justices of the Peace, Etc'. In these books, uniquely, the Hampstead Justices are listed together coherently, all eight of them, with their addresses. In 1890 they are down as 'Hampstead Division', with the JPs all noted to be sitting in the Holborn Division also. In 1894 'St John's Parish, Hampstead' is listed as included in the Holborn Division. But after this a great invisibility descends. The annual listing of Middlesex Justices continued. But the names of those who sat on the Hampstead Bench from 1895 onwards are nowhere among them, even though at the end of the century Hampstead became a full metropolitan borough with its own town hall. Time had indeed forgotten the court – and it flourished.

So, by a happy chance, this present valedictory look at the now extinct West Central Division follows the fortunes of two courts whose distant origins are totally different – the one a tenacious survivor of an ancient, pre-industrial tradition, the other the product of an industrialised, urbanised society responding to the pressures of that change.

3 Old Hampstead

When new magistrates are enrolled in the Commission of the Peace, their training lectures tell them that the office of Justice of the Peace has existed since the 14th century. Like many other impressive pronouncements this is true only in a rather general, figurative way. At different periods Justices have functioned in different ways, constantly changing to suit the needs of the times.

It is true that in 1327 the Parliament of Edward III, responding to a widespread discontent with oppressive sheriffs, enacted a statute which provided that 'in every shire good and lawful men shall be assigned to *keep the peace*', and a number of years later it was stipulated that they should be 'two or three of the best reputation in the counties'; but the role of these very first 'conservators' of the King's Peace was to put down riots and hold periodic courts to control the service and wages of agricultural labourers – really, to keep the peasantry in their place and prevent anarchy at a time when the Black Death had created a serious labour shortage.

Something nearer to the Justices of later centuries emerged in 1361, when further legislation provided that 'in every county in England shall be assigned for the Keeping of the Peace, one Lord, and with him three or four of the most worthy in the county, with some learned in the law.' They were authorised, for the first time, to deal with offenders all the way from pursuit and arrest through to imprisonment, trial and determination of punishment. To help them apprehend offenders they had a few parish constables. Minor transgressions were dealt with summarily; more important ones were taken to a quarterly court which lasted 3–6 days and at which all the Justices appeared together. Here we have the origin of the County Quarter Sessions, which persisted in British criminal justice until 1971 as the next court above the magistrates' court. Serious crimes were dealt with by judges travelling round the kingdom to hold Assize Courts, usually twice a year – again, a system that lasted almost to the present: the various regional Crown Court districts are still referred to as 'circuits'.

No continental European country evolved a system resembling the local magistracy. Across the Channel the rule of law was, for centuries, vested in feudal lords looking down from the turrets of fortified castles, and later in a distant royal or imperial authority without local connections. Britain alone made use of respected local networks in the sovereign's name. Although it was the 'King's Peace' they kept, the King did not interfere with them. These early JPs seem to have been effective in many parts of the country, and if not always liked, trusted. They were not usually great lords but local gentry, often of quite modest family: by the 15th century a JP was merely required to be ordinarily resident in the county in which he sat and to own land there producing at least £20 a year. They were not often corrupt, they had local interests at heart, and they had the confidence of Parliament, which was composed of very much the same class of people.

The one requirement that was seldom met, then or for several centuries to come, was that these magistrates should be 'learned in the law'. However, since most of the offences they dealt with were common-law offences (e.g. assault, robbery, trespass, affray) rather than offences more narrowly defined by statute, common sense and accepted values were probably more useful than a legal training. By the early 17th century the opinion of Sir Edward Coke, Chief Justice of King's Bench, was that 'The whole Christian world hath not the like office as Justice of the Peace if duly executed'.

By then the role of Justice of the Peace had been much enlarged, adding to the duties of the old 'conservators of the peace' other social and administrative tasks. JPs now had in their benevolent or authoritative grasp almost all aspects of County life – which was to say country life, since England was still largely a rural society, with even the county towns serving as service and trading areas for the agricultural lands that ran up to their gates. As a modern legal commentator (Babington) has summarised it: 'They [JPs] regulated wages, prices, profits, employment, marriages, wearing apparel, apprenticeship and house building and even enforced compulsory church attendance on Sundays. Systematically they were put in charge of the regulations dealing with weights and measures, the maintenance of bridges, the licensing of inns, the upkeep of roads, the administration of the Poor Law and the building and control of local prisons.'

In other words, lay magistrates were in charge of the day-to-day running of life, in a world essentially without other bureaucracies and where the infrastructure of local authority as yet consisted largely, in most places, of parish Vestries, what we would now call parish councils, which frequently included the local JPs anyway.

The situation was to remain essentially the same throughout the
17th and 18th centuries and into the 19th, except in London where,
as I have said, the whole system began to break down. Elsewhere,
lay magistrates continued to hold the reins. One early-19th-century
minute book exists for Hampstead; this shows clearly that the
Justices for the district were busy not so much conducting trials
as 'keeping the peace' in a much more general sense, arbitrating in
domestic wrangles, trying to ensure that everyone behaved more or
less within acceptable limits – and watching that ratepayers' money
was not squandered.

Traditionally, local magistrates were supposed to meet in some
public place such as a room over an inn to transact their business.
This probably continued to be the case for their regular weekly or
fortnightly Petty Sessions, when standard issues such as rating
assessments, highway repairs, the licensing of public houses and
workhouse business were usually discussed. However, in the course
of the 18th century, by which time the JPs in affluent areas such as

The lock-up in Cannon Lane, Hampstead

Hampstead tended to be living in imposing houses with plenty of rooms, it seems to have become customary for individual magistrates to hold court, literally, in their own houses to dispose of everyday misdemeanours. Sometimes one of these powerful local figures would invite a colleague or two to join him to arbitrate on the disgraceful conduct of X or the violent altercation between the Y and the Z families. But often, such a man seems to have sat on his own, for convenience or to save time, and he had a right to. Nor was he obliged to have a legal adviser with him such as a local solicitor, or even to keep any records – though some of them did employ clerks, whom they paid out of the fees that then accompanied all summonses. This was in effect a one-man judgement system, unappealable, answerable to no other, dependent on magisterial good will and a high sense of duty if it was not to become a tyranny.

I have not been able to discover who were the principal JPs in Hampstead in the 18th century nor, therefore, where they lived. It is significant, however, that the lock-up set into the high garden wall in Cannon Lane (p 20), which runs below Cannon Hall, a large house near the south-west side of Hampstead Heath, dates from about 1730, some years after the house was built. This strongly suggests the presence of a magistrate at this period in Cannon Hall. Presumably the parish constables or watchmen, if they came upon someone apparently up to no good, would confine them in this lock-up for a few hours, or until the following morning, when the occupant of Cannon Hall had time to deal with them. A flight of stone steps led from the lock-up towards the house, and it is said that the magistrate or magistrates would hold their sessions in what later became the billiard room. Cannon Hall was occupied by successive JPs for decades in the later 19th century (when the lock-up, in fact, had been superseded by police-station cells), almost as if the house bestowed its own privilege and obligation on the tenant. This lasted till 1916, when the property passed into the hands of the actor-manager Gerald du Maurier, hardly the man to sit on the Bench.

Since the earliest registers for Hampstead at London Metropolitan Archives date only from 1880, and a regular run of minute books begins only in 1867, it is a piece of good fortune that one much earlier minute book has survived. It covers a period from mid-May 1827 to October 1831, during the last years of the era during which the patriarchal, all-embracing local role of JPs was at its height. During the six decades that followed, their traditional administrative functions were gradually eroded, as the old Vestries evolved into more elaborate structures of local government, with their elected councils and statutory obligations and powers. So, although the Hampstead Bench, unique in what became the LCC area, did manage to retain its judicial powers and even saw these increase, it progressively lost many of its old duties.

The surviving minute book documents an era which, within the lifetime of many of those concerned, must have come to seem quaintly remote. Much of it is taken up with recording summonses of citizens for non-payment of lamp rates, watch rates, paving rates and poor rates – all these referring to charges for specific amenities agreed by the Hampstead Vestry without reference to what Vestries in other parishes might decide. Parishes were then still far more autonomous than they could be a generation later. In Hampstead, around 1830, pigs and chickens still rooted freely round the back lanes that were muddy or dusty according to season (the Vestry funds did not run to paving except in the main thoroughfares). The water in daily use all came from springs and wells. London, down the hill, had for a long time got much of its water by conduit from the Hampstead ponds, but Hampstead itself was literally above such things. Hampstead had drains, but till the 1840s these went down into the Fleet ditch, thus turning that one-time river into a sewer, and contaminating wells on the lower slopes. The one metropolitan amenity was new-fangled gas lighting up the High Street; elsewhere, there were oil lamps, each individually lit and replenished.

There was as yet no Metropolitan Police Force. Occasional references to 'constables' indicate that there were a few traditional parish constables, but the main protection seems to have been provided by watchmen, also known as 'headboroughs'. A Hampstead resident looking back on his youth from much later in the century wrote: 'These were generally old men for whom no other employment could be found. They only served at night, each man being provided with a rattle and a lanthorn, his station being indicated by a wooden hut or box in which he could take shelter in bad weather.' (Baines, p 164) Watchmen were reputed to use their huts mainly to sleep in, and to be open to bribes to turn a blind eye, but Hampstead's cannot have been totally ineffectual as they had their own watch-house, with two cells, very much like the lock-up at Cannon Hall. This stood on the green at the end of Flask Walk; alongside it were some stocks which seem to have been used for the

At a ~~Special~~ Petty Sessions of his Majesty's Justices of the Peace for the County of Middlesex resident in the Parish of St John Hampstead in the said County holden at the Committee Room in Hampstead Workhouse on Tuesday 15th of May 1827 upon Parochial Business.

Present
Samuel Purkis Esqr in the Chair
Samuel Hoare Esqr

Mr Thomas Toller of the said Parish was appointed Clerk to the Justices in Petty Sessions assembled or to be assembled.

George Thomas in the Employ of Mr Humphreys Wine Merchant of Hampstead was brought up upon a Warrant for refusing to support his Wife, when he was reprimanded in his Wife's presence and afterwards discharged upon his promise to maintain his Wife in future & to pay the Expences sustained by the Parish in relieving his Wife.

Maria Antoinette Ford a Native of France the Mother of an illegitimate Child lately born in the Workhouse was examined in the presence of Charles Thomas Cecil of this Parish Shopman the reputed Father of the Child when an Order of Filiation was made upon Chas T. Cecil – to pay 2£ expences incident to the birth and 2/6 Weekly for the future Maintenance of the Child.

Mary Cornwall of Swaffham Prior Cambridgeshire lately delivered of a Male Bastard Child was examined as to her Settlement but no Order of Removal was made.

Adjourned

Opening page, minute book for 1827–31, Hampstead Justices

last time as late as 1831. The unlucky occupant had got drunk on a Sunday morning and was seen in that state by the vicar. It must have been a magistrate who sentenced him to his punishment.

By the early 19th century, Hampstead's population made it not so much a village as a provincial town. In 1801 it had about 4000 inhabitants, and in 1831 8500. It was to increase relentlessly, reaching 45,000 by 1881 and over 70,000 by 1900. By then, although the Heath and Parliament Hill had been secured as permanent open space, houses had sprouted all over Hampstead. It had become part of London, and certainly part of the LCC area, which makes the Court's achievement in clinging to its special status all the more remarkable.

The first page of the 1827–31 minute book (p 23) is headed: 'At a Petty Sessions of his Magesty's Justices of the Peace for the County of Middlesex resident in the Parish of St John Hampstead in the said County holden at the Committee Room in Hampstead Workhouse on Tuesday 15th of May 1827 upon Parochial Business.' Samuel Purkis, who does not seem to have left other traces in history, was in the Chair, and he was accompanied by Samuel Hoare. This was Samuel Hoare the younger, who married the sister of the prison reformer Elizabeth Fry. Their son John Gurney Hoare became the most prominent campaigner to keep the Heath unbuilt on. Why the book begins on this date is probably revealed by this sentence: 'Mr Thomas Toller of the same Parish was appointed Clerk to the Justices in Petty Sessions assembled or to be assembled.' Perhaps the Bench had decided it was time they kept better records. The same Thomas Toller was appointed the first Clerk to the Vestry, no doubt from a similar motive, 28 years later. He was also, for a long period, Secretary to the copyholders of the manor of Hampstead, and was thus a key figure in the Heath campaign. He continued as Clerk to the Justices till 1868, then retiring from the Vestry also.

From that date on the minute books survive, as if with a change of administration came a new system for keeping paperwork. Under 8 April 1868 we find: 'Mr Thomas Toller having tendered his resignation as Clerk to the Petty Sessions of Hampstead, it was moved by J G Hoare Esq. seconded by Mr James Marshall Esq and Resolved unanimously, That the Justices wish on the retirement of Mr Toller from the Office of Clerk at these Sessions which he has held for 40 years, to record their sense of the knowledge, skill and

judgement with which he has executed his duties and of the
value of the assistance which they have derived from him in the
administration of justice.' Few Justices' Clerks were qualified
lawyers when Toller was appointed; authorities vary on whether
he was a solicitor himself or merely the son of one. The rate books
reveal that he lived for many years at premises listed as 10 Well Walk
– a number shared with the old Pump House and Assembly Rooms,
by then in use as a chapel. With his benign fingers in every local pie,
he sounds a Dickensian figure. I do not know if the Samuel Bush
Toller QC, who figures as a ratepayer around the time that Thomas
was retiring, was a son of his.

When Toller began his long stint, Samuel Purkis, Samuel
Hoare, Charles Bosanquet and William Ballantyne were the JPs
in most frequent attendance. No *ad hoc* hearings in Justices' own
houses figure in this early book; it seems to have been intended
simply to record the regular weekly or fortnightly Petty Sessions.
The Committee Room in Hampstead Workhouse, where they were
held, was by that time in New End in the heart of old Hampstead,
in an old house called Leggatts. Over the next decade, the house
was gradually altered and extended. The building disappeared about
1850 when a soup-kitchen and provident dispensary were erected
at No.16 New End on the site and a new, purpose-built workhouse
infirmary began to rise alongside.

It was logical that the Justices should meet at the workhouse,
since so much court business was bound up with the Poor Law. The
minutes show recurrent concern with the appointment of overseers
and the collection of the poor rate. At this early date, even though
the term 'workhouse' was in regular use, there was not yet the
constant tussle to get a modicum of actual work out of refractory
inmates that shows up in registers later in the century. But here
and in other districts there was a preoccupation with moving some
claimants for workhouse accommodation to their usual 'place of
settlement'. The early correspondence columns of the stodgy but
long-lasting weekly publication *The Justice of the Peace* are full of
searching queries as to whom one might remove and in what
circumstances. The poor, it was much to be regretted, would not
stay in one place. They traipsed about, forming relationships – or
breaking them – in other parishes, and then collapsing there with
children in tow. Perhaps the Hampstead workhouse had a
reputation, amongst the destitute, as a fairly congenial place; at

any rate, one does not read the horror stories about it that were told of the St Pancras workhouse down the hill. The successive 19th-century versions of the Poor Law were often harsh, but in Hampstead individual cases seem to have been looked upon with a modicum of common sense and human decency.

For instance, at the first recorded session in mid-May 1827, there appeared two separate unmarried mothers. One had come from Swaffham Prior in Cambridgeshire; she could not or would not name the father of her child, but no order of removal was made for her. The other, Marie Antoinette Sard, was described as a French citizen; she had had her baby in the workhouse and 'was examined in the presence of Charles Thomas Cecil of this parish, Shopman, the reputed Father of the child.' He was ordered to pay £1 for the birth expenses and 2/6 weekly for the child's keep. Similar cases crop up frequently over the months and 2/6 seems to have been the standard rate for unmarried fatherhood, though late in the year 'a gentleman' was ordered to pay 3/-. Another staple of the court was errant husbands, such as George Thomas, assistant in a wine-merchants' in Hampstead, who in 1827 was 'brought up on a Warrant for refusing to support his Wife, when he was reprimanded in his Wife's presence and afterwards discharged upon his promise to maintain his Wife in future and to pay the Expenses sustained by the Parish in relieving his Wife.' Two years later, in June 1829, another husband was more severely dealt with; presumably his promises had not been kept in the past, since the evidence was stated to have been taken (before William Ballantyne) on a previous occasion. This bricklayer who failed to maintain his wife and child was consigned for 1 month to the House of Correction at Cold Bath Fields in Clerkenwell. This is the only sign in this minute book of the Justices actually sending anyone to prison.

None of the above-mentioned cases would fall within the jurisdiction of an ordinary magistrates' court today. But then, if the Justices spent their time trying to control costs to ratepayers and induce the disreputable to behave like decent citizens, it was partly because there was apparently very little going on in Hampstead that we would recognise as crime. There were a few assaults, one on a constable in July 1828 (fine 10/-, expenses 5/-), and another in which a woman attacked another 'in the Cow Yard' and was bound over to keep the peace in her own recognisance of £5 and another surety of £5 put up by someone else. (£5 was a not inconsiderable sum in

those days, but of course the money would have to be produced
only if the subject caused more trouble.)

Binding over was quite frequent since, by old tradition, the
magistrates were there to keep the peace for the good of all rather
than delving into the history of individual quarrels, and in a world
where there were no police to take up the cause of a complainant,
and taking out a summons cost money, ordinary people would
think several times before embarking on litigation. There was the
occasional case of drunkenness, though I have not managed to find
in the record the celebrated drunk who was the alleged last occupant
of the stocks. Another case, on 21 August 1827, echoes even more
strongly the 17th-century world in which the roots of the magistracy
lay. Isaac Hicks the younger (even the name seems redolent of
Puritan times) 'was convicted. . . for exercising his worldly calling
on Sunday. . .Not to be enforced upon his promising to pay the fine
due upon a former conviction under the same Act.' The nature of
the calling is not specified.

In December 1828 a number of tradesmen were fined, mainly
1/6 each, for having weights and measures that were slightly
deficient. Such cases, along with rates defaulters, were the regular
fare of the sessions. The Hampstead Justices quite often remitted
rates if the man summoned had a good many children to feed. Yet
every now and again into this benign, self-sufficient society comes
a hint of something bleaker. In the same month Samuel Purkis and
Samuel Hoare heard the evidence of a girl who had been in the
charge of the parish in the Orphan Working School, and had been
apprenticed under the usual Poor Law provisions 2 months before
to a James Clarke, a tradesman in the High Street. The girl 'stated
upon her oath that her Master frequently beat her particularly on
Sunday the 10th instant and on the following Sunday, and that he
had tied her to the bedstead for several hours together.' The
accusations were corroborated by the neighbours. Complaints from
masters about apprentices who had made off were more in the usual
line of the court's business; it is encouraging to read that on this
occasion the magistrates cancelled the apprenticeship and ordered
that half the premium paid to Clarke was to be returned to the
coffers of the parish. He was also to return 17/- belonging to the girl
'of which he had taken possession', but of what happened to either
of the parties afterwards there is no record. One likes to think that,
in a place where everyone knew everyone else's business, Clarke's

behaviour, with its hint of indecency as well as violence, was long remembered.

It would have been the Bench who had apprenticed this girl in the first place, since that duty too still fell within the Justices' remit. In October 1829, for example, we hear of two boys being bound apprentice, one, aged 13, to a ladies' shoemaker living off Maiden Lane near Battle Bridge, and the other, at only 9, going to a chimney sweep in the parish of St Giles-in-the-Fields. Presumably he was to be a little climbing boy, since this was not illegal till 1840 and in practice continued for many years longer. Was there, one wonders, any regular follow-up by the Justices as to how these children were treated in the parishes to which they were consigned? The other noteworthy thing about this entry is that, for the first time, Purkis was sitting along with a magistrate called Benjamin Edward Hall. The lists of Middlesex Justices reveal that Hall later lived at Paddington Green, and I believe that he was the Sir Benjamin Hall who, as an older man, became MP for Marylebone, and was, for some time, implacably opposed to unifying London's heterogeneous local government bodies. However, his mind was changed by a cholera epidemic in the early 1850s and, seeing the necessity for a centralised public health system, he was one of the original designers of what became the Metropolitan Board of Works in 1856.

As for Purkis, a small mystery attends him. Unlike his fellow Justices, he does not figure in Pigot's London Directory of the period under the listing 'Nobility, Gentry and Clergy', nor does his name crop up as a Hampstead ratepayer. Since the surviving Justices' lists date only from 1842, it is not particularly surprising that they do not include his name. The last entry in the Hampstead minute book was made on 15 October 1831 and much, including death, can supervene in 11 years. But did his death, I wonder, come more suddenly and dramatically than that? The handwriting throughout this minute book is identical and I suspect that it is his, since he was almost always in the Chair. There is only one occasion in 4½ years when his name does not appear, and as no one else is mentioned in the Chair on that day this may be an omission. Conversely, it is clear from numerous gaps in time that a good many other sessions took place which must have been recorded in a different book or books which have not survived. In other words, I believe this book was his own record and it ends with disconcerting abruptness. On 15 October, during a bread-and-butter administrative session, sums of money needed to repair the highways were being discussed. It is stated that the Justices gave their assessment as – and then the record breaks off in mid-sentence, indeed in mid pen-stroke. All the rest of the pages in the book are blank. Did Samuel Purkis actually collapse on the Bench that morning in the old workhouse in New End?

Apart from the possibility of such domestic drama, the peace of the magistrates themselves was disturbed in these years only by the passing of Robert Peel's Metropolitan Police Act in 1829. For the first time there was instituted a London-wide force, independent of the parishes and boroughs – though excluding the City, which had its own officers, as it does to this day. Work began in the spring of 1830 on assembling this first police force, initially 3300 men, many of them recruited among ex-soldiers. They were given a smart uniform – blue cutaway with white buttons, leather stock, stovepipe hat and truncheon – and the intention was that by their sheer presence on the streets they would deter crime as well as arresting criminals. Not everyone, however, was enthusiastic about the idea. There were fears, which turned out to be groundless, of 'police tyranny' and spying, as was the style across the Channel. The new officers were warned by their superiors to proceed cautiously 'with every moderation and forbearance.' Many of the earliest constables were dismissed for failing to reach this high standard, and especially for being drunk on duty. Very few, however, seem to have been corrupt.

The Hampstead Vestry and Justices had a more particular objection to the new police; they feared the loss of Hampstead's status as a separate town. At a meeting on 11 November 1830 the Vestry passed a motion to 'Represent the unnecessary application of the Metropolitan Police to this parish, as at present there is not wanted more vigilance than our former system of watching produced under our local Act of Parliament; and as it increases our burthen of taxation by upwards of eleven hundred pounds per annum we humbly request the same police may be withdrawn at the close of the first year.' They followed this up with a deputation to Peel in the Home Office, but their careful explanation that their previous expenses of £577.16.10 (including £26.12.6 for watchmen's candles) were now replaced by 'the enormous sum of £1,615.6.8' had no effect, and the police remained in Hampstead. By 1838 there

were eight constables working in shifts out of a house at the top of
Holly Hill, locally derided for following an occupation not thought
to be necessary. This was shortly before the Metropolitan Police
Courts Act of 1839, which renamed the public offices of paid
magistrates 'police courts', and added to their number. Hampstead,
though, managed to avoid being included in these arrangements
(see chapter 2), on the grounds that the place was too peaceful to
warrant such an establishment.

By and by, Hampstead became attached to its police force,
especially once the Easter fair on the Heath began to attract large
numbers of riotous Londoners. It was even recorded late in the
century that 'gallant acts have been done by the police in
Hampstead, and their bearing and discipline have been at all
times unexceptionable.'

Meanwhile, what of the early days of Clerkenwell Court, only
3 miles away towards London, but socially a world away?

It will be recalled (see chapter 2) that the district of Clerkenwell
received one of the first public offices, with a full-time magistrate
in attendance, before the end of the 18th century. For most of its
first 50 years this office was situated to the south of the district,
at 54 Hatton Garden in Holborn. No records survive from it and
no plaque marks its place. Fortunately, this was part of Dickens's
familiar territory and he has created an unforgettable, grotesque
memorial to it in *Oliver Twist*. In chapter XI the Artful Dodger,
having stolen Mr Brownlow's handkerchief outside a bookshop
near Clerkenwell Green, contrives to turn the pursuing cries of
'Stop thief!' against Oliver and it is Oliver who is dragged into the
presence of Mr Fang, the Hatton Garden magistrate.

> The office was a front parlour, with a panelled wall. Mr Fang sat
> behind a bar, at the upper end; and on one side of the door was
> a sort of wooden pen in which poor little Oliver was already
> deposited; trembling very much at the awfulness of the scene.
>
> Mr Fang was a lean, long-backed, stiff-necked, middle-sized
> man, with no great quantity of hair, and what he had, growing on
> the back and sides of his head. His face was stern and much
> flushed. If he were really not in the habit of drinking rather more
> than was exactly good for him, he might have brought an action
> against his countenance for libel, and have recovered heavy
> damages...
>
> Now, it so happened that Mr Fang was at that moment
> perusing a leading article in a newspaper of the morning,
> adverting to some recent decision of his, and commending him,
> for the three hundredth and fiftieth time, to the special and
> particular notice of the Secretary of State for the Home
> Department. He was out of temper; and he looked up with
> an angry scowl.

It is clear that Dickens is presenting us with an unsparing,
satirical portrait of an actual magistrate. Mr Fang insults everyone,
in particular the luckless and extremely gentlemanly Mr Brownlow;

he seems to have only the vaguest grasp of who is appearing in his court in what role, and both his clerk and his gaoler have learnt to cough or drop heavy books at appropriate moments to smother his more preposterous threats. Even the thief-taker ('a bluff old fellow in a striped waistcoat, who was standing by the bar') appears kindly and sensible compared with his superior, pointing out that Oliver seems genuinely ill and is in no state to answer questions. When a supporting arm is removed from him, Oliver collapses on the floor:

> The men in the office looked at each other, but no one dared
>   to stir.
> "I knew he was shamming," said Fang, as if this were
>   incontestable proof of the fact.
> "Let him lie there. He'll soon be tired of that."
> "How do you propose to deal with the case, sir?" inquired
>   the clerk in a low voice.
> "Summarily," replied Mr Fang. "He stands committed for three
>   months – hard labour of course. Clear the office."'

Fortunately, in the nick of time, the bookseller rushes in with his very different side of the story, since he saw that it was not Oliver but another boy who committed the theft.

> "What is this? Who is this? Turn this man out. Clear the office!"
>   cried Mr Fang. "I *will* speak," cried the man; "I will not be
>   turned out. I saw it all. I keep the book-stall. I demand to be
>   sworn. I will not be put down. Mr Fang, you must hear me.
>   You must not refuse, sir."
> The man was right. His manner was determined; and the matter
>   was growing rather too serious to be hushed up. "Swear the
>   man," growled Mr Fang, with a very ill grace.
> "Now, man, what have you got to say?"

The matter is finally put right; the magistrate, losing his way again, resorts to threatening Mr Brownlow with prosecution for neglecting to pay for a book which he still happens to be holding in his hand, but eventually Oliver is swept off by Brownlow in a coach, to a different life. Fang is a typical Dickens caricature, but anyone who has frequented magistrates' courts up to and including the present day will recognise elements of Fang in the occasional full-time magistrate. It has often been observed that the isolation in which many stipendiaries conduct their business, unlike either lay magistrates or Crown Court judges, is not necessarily conducive to good decisions, and that over-familiarity with the Court's grinding daily round of human folly readily leads to contempt. As G K Chesterton said, the full-time magistrate, faced with an unending procession of mainly petty offenders, almost inevitably ceases to see them as varied individuals since they all just become 'the usual man in the usual place'.

Dickens was clearly on a mission in this chapter: 'Although the presiding Genii in such an office as this exercise a summary and arbitrary power over the liberties, the good name, the character, almost the lives, of Her Majesty's subjects, especially of the poorer class. . . they are closed to the public, except through the medium of the daily press.' Or, he could have added, the medium of novels by hugely successful writers. It seems unlikely, from their name, that the public offices were officially closed to the general public, but it may well have been that autocratic Genii did their best to make this the case ('Mr Fang. . . was not a little indignant to see an unbidden guest enter.') In fact, Dickens was writing in 1837–8, near the end of the era of Hatton Garden. Within 2 years, the Metropolitan Police Courts Act had been passed, and purpose-built courts were going up in several places, including Clerkenwell, with the public in mind.

What became of Mr Fang? His real name was Allen Stewart Laing. He was a barrister of the Temple who had previously practised at the Bar as an equity draftsman, so why he was ever thought suitable to the daily rough-and-tumble of a magistrates' court it is hard to say. However, he may have been more convivial among his own kind than he appeared when embattled in Hatton Garden. One remembers Dickens's gibe about his drinking. At any rate, he was for a while an assiduous attender at the Magistrates' Dining Club, which met at the Middlesex Sessions House when Quarter Sessions or other notable events were taking place (2/6 a time, 'including dessert', and wine by subscription, but ginger beer, soda water, coffee or tea extra). In 1837 and 1838 his signature appears, usually on top of the list, in the soot-rimmed pages of a handsome leather-bound 'dinner book' which has survived. Perhaps he was a rather lonely man. As Dickens indicates, his arbitrary decisions were indeed often criticised in *The Times*, and perhaps his being recognisably satirised in *Oliver Twist* was the last straw.

Accounts vary as to whether he retired from the Metropolitan Bench soon afterwards or whether the Home Secretary actually dismissed him. It is an irony that he is now the only remembered representative of his calling, when a large body of more distinguished practitioners have passed into oblivion.

Hatton Garden must have seemed a logical site in the 1790s when the public office was set up there, for it was already a densely populated area that had gone down socially since it had first been laid out with houses in the 17th century. There was also something of a tradition of law enforcement in the area, which was so near to the City as to be geographically part of it but outside its jurisdiction. A few streets east of Hatton Garden had stood, since 1612, Hicks Hall, which for the next 180 years was the Sessions House for Middlesex, where Middlesex Justices sat and trials were held quarterly before judge and jury. It was a handsome brick house with a stone portico and large, mullioned windows which was the gift of a wealthy and public-spirited silk merchant and financier, Sir Baptist Hicks JP, who thought justice ought not to be enacted in noisy rooms over taverns. It stood in the middle of the road near the southern end of St John Street, with its own roundhouse (lock-up) and pillory alongside. By the late 18th century the building was dilapidated and its situation near Smithfield meat market had in its turn become too noisy and lacking in dignity. After 1782 it was pulled down, to be replaced by a new building further north, at the western end of Clerkenwell Green, but this second Sessions House was long called by the same name as the old one.

As we have seen, Mr Laing, along with other metropolitan magistrates, attended Quarter Sessions. Some of Hampstead's Justices would no doubt have sat there too, as was their right. But they would have found themselves under the chairmanship of a full-time lawyer, later always a judge. For this reason, among others, Quarter Sessions in the London area soon ceased to be the high point of the year that provincial Quarter Sessions were for the rural JPs. The Sessions House was much altered and extended in the late 19th century. It stands to this day (p 35), no longer a court of law but a Masonic administrative headquarters.

The area was also traditionally one of prisons, destination of some of the defendants passing through the local magistrates' courts. Three ancient prisons, Newgate, Bridewell and the Fleet prison, had stood on or near the banks of the Fleet for centuries, each at various times destroyed and rebuilt. A little further north in Clerkenwell a new and more spacious House of Correction was constructed in 1794 on part of Cold Bath Fields (now the site of Mount Pleasant postal sorting office). In addition, a little way behind Clerkenwell Green stood the local gaol, the House of Detention for Middlesex. First erected in 1615, it was rebuilt several times, the last one in the mid-1840s after the opening of the new police court building in Bagnigge Wells Road. It was heavily damaged by a Fenian bomb in 1867 and pulled down 10 years later when the control of prisons became centralised. Its original doorway, with a grotesque stone head (of a hanged man?) over it still stands in a lane off Sans Walk. The underground cells survived beneath a local authority school built on the site, and in recent years have been turned into a museum.

In the 1840s there was much concentration on the reorganisation and institutionalisation of law and order; at the same period many new, purpose-built workhouses appeared, including the one in New End, Hampstead. The 'public offices' were renamed Police Courts because in future, instead of employing

Former Sessions House, Clerkenwell Green (1785)

their own constables they were to come under the umbrella of the Metropolitan Police, established 10 years earlier. The new name unfortunately created the impression that the courts were run by and for the police rather than in the public interest. This lasted a full 100 years, till after World War II, and although the older and more general term Magistrates' Court was then officially substituted for Police Court, the aura of the police still hung about it and persists to this day, partly because metropolitan police courts were all designed to incorporate a police station, or subsequently acquired one alongside.

Two police *stations* were set up in the Clerkenwell police district when the Metropolitan Police were formed. One was a cramped office actually inside the King's Cross monument at the crossroads at the top of Gray's Inn Road. The other was enlarged from an old watchhouse in Rosoman Street, on land acquired from the New River Company. (Finsbury Town Hall was later to be built on the site.) When the new police court was opened in Bagnigge Wells Road, the Rosoman Street officers moved over there into purpose-built accommodation. The Victorian sense of the power, wealth and

Clerkenwell Magistrates' Court, King's Cross Road (1906) from the north-west

dignity of office was getting into its stride. There was a feeling that the cramped police offices established in ordinary terrace houses were 'not at all worthy of a great city like London and the important space they fill in the public eye.' (Grant)

Today, across King's Cross Road from the junction with Acton Street, stands the now closed Magistrates' Court, an imposing 1906 building showing John Dixon Butler's 'bold use of Free Classical elements' (Pevsner) (p 36). Adjoining it, sandwiched between it and a mid-Victorian police station (now disused), is a modest two-storey block in early Victorian brick and stucco, with the royal coat of arms sculpted above a gateway (*below*). This building is what remains of the original court house, and was in fact the part of it that served as police accommodation, complete with charge room, gaoler's bedroom and a long line of cells in the yard to the rear, where a second courtroom was later built. Part of the original courthouse, which was in the same style, was demolished to make way for the large main building that is there now. The small, recessed portion like a bridge between the old and new buildings spans what was

The same court from the south-west, showing the surviving block of the 1842 courthouse on the right, with royal coat of arms over the near gateway

once the main vehicle entrance through the old building to the stable yard behind.

In the houses such as those in Bow Street and Hatton Garden that were made over as courts, the prisoners, witnesses, magistrates and court staff all had to come and go by the same entrance, often pushing their way through a crowd of interested onlookers. Dickens's *Sketches by Boz* include a description of the prisoners' van leaving, with a convicted teenage girl playing to the gallery: "Don't you be in a hurry, coachman. . .and recollect, I want to be set down in Cold Bath Fields – a large house with a high garden wall in front: you can't mistake it." In courts such as Clerkenwell designed by Charles Reeves (who subsequently became the first Metropolitan Police Surveyor and designed a number of courts) more convenient arrangements were installed, with more privacy for everyone. Prisoners could now be brought to and from the court via a yard that was not open to the public and had its own way straight into

Interior of Court 1, Clerkenwell, circa 1910. When the courthouse closed in 1998 little had changed physically except that the early-electric chandelier had been replaced with more modern lighting, and a telephone had appeared

to the courtroom through the turnkey's office. One of the two front entrances on the court side was for the magistrates and clerks, while the other, for the public and witnesses, led past the waiting room and the warrant office to the courtroom itself.

This (p 38) was described in the *Illustrated London News* 5 years after the Clerkenwell court had opened as

> a larger one than most of the 'Worthy Magistrates' are blessed with – in fact, a handsome, airy, wainscoted apartment. You glance at once toward the judicial armchair, and see it faced and flanked by the usual police Court arrangements – a square, open box in the centre, bounded, so to speak, on one side by the Bench, on the others by the particular boxes occupied by Clerks, Police Inspectors, Reporters, Barristers, and last, not least, Culprits. The part of the room not taken up by these pens and boxes forms the *locus standi* for that portion of the enlightened public who come to improve their tempers by the contemplation of the placid equanimity of a Greenwood – or to see how perfectly even the balance of justice, as between a private individual and a policeman can be held by a Combe.

Greenwood and Combe were the resident magistrates, of whom we shall hear more shortly. It is clear that a heavy irony has now taken over. Indeed, the tone of mockery has already been set by the introductory paragraphs: a general, unfocused condemnation of all concerned pervades the article:

> In Bagnigge Wells Road – the bottom of that valley which separates the sloping squares and terraces of Pentonville – a region of very green house doors, and very bright knockers, and intensely red brick facings – from the more ancient and solemn looking streets which abut upon the western side of Gray's Inn Lane – in that glaring and dusty summer thoroughfare stands a large pile of buildings, generally ornamented by numerous lounging policemen, and further diversified and adorned by crowds of shabby-looking people, a vast proportion whereof may be observed to have their personal appearance improved by such additional attractions as are contributed by blackened eyes, plastered up foreheads and noses with broken bridges. . .
> We enter – we traverse a long, dirty passage: the passages to Police Courts are always dirty – the walls are always greasy – glazed, so to speak, by the constant friction of frowsty rags.

(The building, at this point, had only been open for five years, and it is likely that the journalist's strictures about its state were as exaggerated as his view of the Clerkenwell population.)

> A turn to the left – a push at a swinging door – and we stand in the midst of a similar crowd to that which we left outside, to that which we passed in the lobby – the disreputable public of a Police Court.

This, then, is to be the writer's theme: the sordid, disgraceful yet pitiable *otherness* of people who frequent police courts as opposed to the decent, respectable, soap-using, newspaper-reading rest of the population. (No wonder, one may feel, that the burghers of Hampstead felt insulted at the very idea that a police court might be established in their parish!) This voyage-to-the-lower-depths tone, unknown in the pre-Victorian era, became increasingly common as the century went by, and as the ever-enlarging commercial middle class began to live in a segregated comfort, gentility and conscious piety unknown to its fathers. The tone, originally adopted by Dickens in his set-piece descriptions of the rookeries of St Giles', finds expression in Mayhew's interviews with labouring Londoners in the 1860s, in Charles Bradlaugh's and W T Stead's crusading journalism in the 1870s and 1880s, in William Booth's *Darkest London* in 1890, and in Compton Mackenzie's defining novel *Sinister Street*, published just before the first World War. If taken entirely literally – and many subsequent social historians have done so – these shocked details would convince the reader that a real social abyss then separated the upper (and even middle) classes from the lower, and that the poverty and degradation of the latter were unique to the times. A little research soon indicates that this was not true – that infinite gradations lay between intense respectability and its opposite extreme, and that in an area like Clerkenwell huge numbers of more or less decent ordinary citizens managed to live out their lives its narrow streets just as they had in every London district for centuries. But this would hardly have suited the lip-smacking, revelatory aim of the *Illustrated London News* writer – one Angus B Reach.

> We have mentioned the general character of the district over which the Clerkenwell Court exercises its police control. Many of our readers are no doubt familiar with the densely peopled, dirty, confused, huddled locality, which stretches around the Middlesex

Sessions House. Many of them have, we doubt not, been bewildered amid its dingy, swarming alleys – have emerged from its squalid courts, crowded with tattered, sodden-looking women, and hulking unwashed men – clustering round the doors of low-browed public-houses; or seated by dingy, unwindowed shops, frowsy with piles of dusty, ricketty rubbish; or reeking with the odour of coarse food – lumps of carrion-like meat simmering in greasy pans, and brown, crusty-looking morsels of fish, still gluey with the oil in which they have been fried – many of our readers, we say, have probably congratulated themselves, with a cosy, self-satisfied shrug, as they emerged from these odoriferous haunts into the broad and frequented thoroughfare, where the shops do not look dens, nor the passengers ruffians and sluts.

In Clerkenwell, there is grovelling starving poverty. In Clerkenwell broods the darkness of utter ignorance. In its lanes and alleys the lowest debauch – the coarsest enjoyment – the most infuriate passions – the most unrestrained vice - roar and riot –

And so on and so forth. Fences, pickpockets, 'half-starved Italian minstrels' and Irish hodmen figure; so do low public houses where thieves 'drink and smoke' (what could be baser?); so do 'Jew receivers, with sharp leering eyes' and 'brazen, ragged women' who 'scream and shout ribald repartee from window to window. . .' The writer pauses only for a mild jeer in passing at the 'poor shabby-genteel City missionary', evidently outclassed by the vicious excitements by which he is surrounded. (London City Missionaries were an inter-denominational organisation, dedicated to bringing the gospel to the English equivalent of heathen savages.) He continues:

The judicial capital of such a district – the Clerkenwell Police Court – of necessity reveals many a murderous outrage – many a daring robbery – many a case of lingering, untended starvation – many a death struggle between the sleuth hounds of the police and the housebreaker, tracked step by step, hunted from place to place, and at length trapped like a wild beast in his lair.

What these ravening beasts found to rob within convenient range of Clerkenwell Court, a district which then, as 70 years later, contained few houses worth breaking into and little worth stealing, is not clear. The passage seems suffused by some more general, unsubstantiated perception of social anarchy, probably because

Clerkenwell Green itself had a long history as a site for mass meetings of a radical kind – banned there in 1842. Ten years earlier, Cold Bath Fields had also known a mass demonstration, in the course of which one of Peel's new policemen was killed.

The article concludes more calmly:

'Mr Combe is a jolly-faced, homely, country-gentleman-looking personage. He is one of the common-sense, in opposition to the legal technicality-loving magistrates. He is a frank, kind-hearted man, with a lurking penchant for the turf – a good

Mr Greenwood, resident magistrate at Clerkenwell police court, and (above) Mr Combe (*Illustrated London News*, 22 May 1847)

judge of a spanking team, and if reports speak truly, a crack whip.
As may be expected, with these qualifications, he looks after the
cabmen pretty strictly – understands all their manoeuvres – is a
capital judge of fares – and down upon an omnibus man in a
moment, either for racing or loitering.'

Here, incidentally, comes an early hint of those traffic offences
which, a century or so later, swelled into a major part of the court's
work – a great, unwieldy mass of obscure prosecutions burdening an
adversarial system that was never framed to deal with them. Boyce
Combe, for such was his name (p 42, above) lived in Gower Street
and also had an establishment at Acton, then perhaps in splendid
open countryside for horsey pursuits.

John Beswicke Greenwood (p 42, below) lived nearby in
Woburn Square. He was, according to Angus B Reach,

> 'a Yorkshireman – a hard, tetchy, irritable, high dried Whig.
> The *Times* and the *Examiner*, in particular, have kept a sharp look
> out upon him; and his decisions have given rise to many a bitter
> article.'

We seem to have here another Fang figure, with the difference that,
while Dickens was content to satirise and fictionalise his prey, Reach
attacks a public figure in a remarkably full-frontal way one could
hardly get away with today. However, methods similar to Reach's
seem to have worked, since a footnote to the article tells us that
'Within these few days, Mr Greenwood has voluntarily resigned his
appointment' – thus completing his resemblance to the notorious
Laing nine years earlier.

After such a lurid tour round Clerkenwell, it comes as quite
a relief to hear that 'Mr Mallet, the Chief Clerk, is a quiet,
gentlemanly man; Mr R Mould, his subaltern, a lawyer of no
inconsiderable knowledge and research.' Already, we seem to have
travelled a long way from the ignorant, venial, legally unadvised
Middlesex magistrates of the late 18th century. Indeed, the whole
administration of justice had altered since the beginning of the
1820s. Under both Tory and Whig influences, capital punishment
was abolished for scores of relatively minor crimes of dishonesty,
and transportation for life was a thing of the past soon after 1850.
Many indictable offences, since they no longer attracted savage
punishments, even in theory, were removed from the jury trials of

Quarter Sessions and Assizes to the summary jurisdiction of the magistrates' courts.

These courts, once in operation, were kept busy. The middle decades of the 19th century saw a mass of new legislation, some of it codifying and detailing acts that had always been common-law offences, but much of it creating new ones. Laws came in to regulate alehouses, common lodging houses, bath-houses, slaughterhouses, pawnbrokers and theatres. Attempts were made to exercise more control over gaming, dancing, street trading, peddling, vagrancy, homelessness, markets and fairs. 'Drunk and disorderly' became a formal and frequent charge. So did public indecency, though this did not always indicate sexual activity: in some places and circumstances 'indecent behaviour' might amount to no more than catcalling or playing leap-frog. Master–servant relationships came under greater scrutiny, along with traditional 'perks' of certain jobs which were now stigmatised as 'theft'. Pauper children, lunatics, dogs, blood sports, burial grounds, wells, poisonous substances, vaccination, hackney carriages, public nuisances and 'offensive trades' all began to receive an attention which they had previously escaped. Sunday trading became a particular preoccupation, and maypoles were discouraged for decades. Even ice-slides made on pavements in cold weather became subject to the law.

All this attempted control was a mark of rising standards of public order rather than the reverse, but the police were cautious in trying to implement some of the new laws. The suppression of traditional fairs, such as the Hampstead Heath one, was a particularly unpopular measure that was later abandoned. At the end of the 18th century the annual Hampstead Fair had been at 'West End', today's West Hampstead. This had been shut down by the Bench, determined to keep the rougher side of London at bay, after a particularly riotous occasion in 1819 when professional gangs of robbers had moved in. However, the Fair re-emerged at a site on the Heath, and finally settled at its present location near South End Green.

In general, the coming of the Metropolitan Police did have the desired calming effect on the streets of London; no longer were respectable elderly gentleman like Mr Brownlow in such constant danger of losing their handkerchiefs or watches. In fact, the prevalence of actual crime seems to have been in inverse ratio to the number of emotive newspaper tirades about the notorious 'vice' of areas such as Clerkenwell. James Grant, whose *Sketches in London* appeared 8 years after Peel's officers first came onto the streets and who knew the courts well, wrote: 'With respect to crimes against the person, they are now comparatively rare. Everyone, in fact, who lives in London feels a consciousness of security, both in regard to his person and property, which was not felt before the establishment of the new police. Person and property are now incomparably safer than they were under the old system. . .The new police are now the objects of universal approbation, and deservedly so.'

More meditative observers noted that it was remarkable the way the police had achieved sufficient moral authority to subdue a vast mass of people, most of whom were not so much 'depraved' as simply ignorant, poor and free of the Victorian middle-class preoccupation with sin. Indeed, the fear of crime seems to have related for most of the century more to a generalised unease about the growing differences between classes than to any real threat to bourgeois comfort. A half-formed awareness of the vulnerability of the prosperous to mob violence lurked in the background. There was much use of the term 'the criminal classes', but Grant's view was that though there had formerly been a large mass of people in London living by dishonesty, whole worlds of Artful Dodgers, 'now, I will venture to say. . .that the amount of property yearly stolen in London does not amount to £100,000; and that the number of regular thieves, or those who live by theft, is under 5000.'

One modern authority on crime (George Rudé) has estimated that perhaps only 10% of offences between 1835 and 1860 were committed by professional criminals. The rest were attributable to people who were normally in work but who just occasionally stole or got into a fight – citizens who were not perhaps models of respectability but who were far from being the denizens of the night of popular and enduring imagination.

5 Hampstead's new police station

In April 1867, a year before Mr Toller, the long-serving clerk to the Justices, retired, a new Hampstead minutes of evidence book was started. This was the one that, 12 months later, recorded the Bench's gratitude to Toller and the ending of an era, for when the next book opens, the magistrates are stated for the first time to be sitting in 'The Police Court, Rosslyn Hill'. As we know, Hampstead, with its entirely lay Bench, was never a 'police court' in the strict sense of the term, but I assume the fact of its being accommodated from 1868 within Hampstead's police station was enough for the name to be loosely used.

A quarter of a century after the inauguration of the first purpose-built police courts, among them Clerkenwell, another round of reorganisation and reconstruction began. The Metropolitan Board of Works, the body that was to grow into the London County Council, had been founded in 1856; during the 1860s it acquired more powers. New Boards of Poor Law Guardians were set up, separate from the Vestries. Justices of the Peace were gradually losing the patriarchal administrative functions that had occupied them in the past; with the formation of the LCC in 1888 the only administrative functions that would remain were overseeing the weights and measures of local tradesmen, and control over public houses and other places where alcohol was sold.

But in other directions the work of magistrates' courts, and hence of the Hampstead Justices and all other Justices outside London, was expanding. Important Acts of 1847 and '48 conferred on their Petty Sessions the same role as formal courts, with greater rights to try without jury cases that would formerly have gone to Quarter Sessions. This paved the way for the situation we still have today, in which all cases come up initially before magistrates, in hearings regulated by statute. Along with these changes went an increased concern for justice not only to be done but to be seen to be done. The old, briskly informal way of JPs conducting business at home was now deemed inadequate, as was the scanty record-keeping. At the beginning of 1852 *The Justice of the Peace*, which was evidently now being read by large numbers of magistrates anxious to acquire an appropriate gravitas and concern for due process, published a letter expressing their current anxieties:

'Can the magistrates of a municipal borough. . .legally at their
residence summarily convict persons of offences (vagrancy, for instance)
and, if so should not the evidence be taken on oath and proper minutes
made thereof?. . .Should not legally all cases of summary conviction be
heard and determined in open court and in such a place as a police office,
and would the convictions be bad, and the justice be liable to an action
for such convictions at his residence, a fit and proper place having been
provided by the town council?'

The answer, from one of the panel of lawyers whose
contributions made up the weekly paper, was fairly reassuring.
Provided there was open access to the hearing and that the oaths
were properly taken 'we doubt whether a conviction would be bad
on the single ground of its having been made at the magistrate's
private residence instead of at the police office. . .There is nothing
in the act which, so far as we see, renders it compulsory on the
magistrates to act there [i.e. in the place provided by the town
council] if they choose to sit elsewhere within the borough.'

The following year further powers to try assault cases were
given to Justices and in 1855 their jurisdiction was extended over
all cases of simple larceny. The Justices' Clerks Society, holding
their first general meeting 'under the new rules' at the Law Society
in Chancery Lane (as befitted their enhanced status as advisors
to JPs with new powers) were asked to submit their comments.
The subject of when a court was truly a court was again paraded:

> It was debated whether the important judicial functions proposed
> to be conferred by the new bill should not be limited to the
> Justices assembled in petty sessions for the division at the usual
> place for holding the sessions, in order to clothe such tribunal
> with as much of the attributes of a court of justice as possible, but
> it was considered by some that practical difficulties might occur
> by such a restriction in certain localities. . .

Indeed, the idea that, in the 1850s, whatever local authority
existed would have already bestirred itself to provide 'a fit and
proper place' for its magistrates, seems premature, unless 'fit and
proper' was to be interpreted very liberally. (The Greenwich Justices,
for instance, were still meeting near the end of the century in a room
above a public house.) I assume the Hampstead Justices were still in
their workhouse accommodation in the 1850s and indeed till the late

1860s, since I have found no trace of them elsewhere. But it
equally seems entirely consistent with the changing times, and the
appointment of separate Poor Law Guardians, that the JPs should
have moved into accommodation in the new police station that
was opened in 1868. According to F E Baines, an old Hampstead
resident writing late in the century, the court occupied a specifically
designated room and sat every week. For the first time, prisoners
kept in police cells could be brought straight up into the court
rather than being marched through the streets to the workhouse.

The station was built on Rosslyn Hill in front of the Royal
Soldiers' Daughters' Home, just where the present side lane to
Greenhill begins to rise and Rosslyn Hill becomes the High Street:
a wall fountain marks the fact that it was the site of the ancient
Red Lion tavern. The police station (*below*) was a four-square, three-
storey brick building with stone dressings, typical of its time, with
what were probably stables alongside. It ceased to be a police station
in 1913, when another was built as part of the complex including
a proper magistrates' court on the corner of Downshire Hill (p 49).
A modern 'mews' development, Mulberry Close, now occupies the
site, but the station's old, low front wall, stepped to accommodate

The 1867 Police Station at the top of Rosslyn Hill, Hampstead, where the
magistrates were provided with a room for their sittings. The building has been
demolished and a new development fills the site, but the low, stepped wall
remains to this day

the steep slope of the road at that point, is still there.

John Gurney Hoare, son of Samuel, residing at Child's Hill to the north-west of Hampstead, was socially the grandest Hampstead justice of the 1860s and by then the most senior: he was born in 1810 and was appointed to the Bench in succession to his father in 1841. No doubt this was why he put in an appearance to bid formal farewell to Mr Toller; otherwise, his name does not very often appear in the minutes. (His younger brother, Joseph, was appointed in 1869.) The most assiduous and prominent JPs of the 1860s and '70s were Joseph Read, who lived in a large house off Haverstock Hill, and James Marshall, later a founder-member of the LCC, who lived near North End, then bought Cannon Hall (*cf.* chapter 3) from the previous owner in the late 1860s and lived there till the early '80s, when he moved to Grosvenor Street. I think it is Marshall's rapid scrawl that fills most of the minute books of the period – minutes of evidence, whether kept by magistrate or clerk, are commonly scrawled, since they are required to be a rapid longhand memo of testimony given verbatim. Only now and then, usually as the preliminary statement of charges, does a neat, clerkly copperplate supervene.

Hampstead Magistrates' Court (John Dixon Butler, 1913), with police station beyond

The entries for 1867 and '68 are still fairly sparse compared with those in later volumes. The Court sat once or at most twice a week, since these northern heights did not suffer the daily profusion of petty crime that afflicted an urban area such as Clerkenwell. Much of the land bordering Haverstock Hill, the southern reaches of Hampstead, had yet to be laid out in streets, and, to the north, the future Hampstead Garden Suburb and Golders Green was still open country and would be into the next century. On the other hand, and for the same reason, the jurisdiction of Hampstead Court was geographically much wider than it would be in later decades, and included not only Highgate but the fields and farms of Hendon. So what one has is a record that still appears to speak of a country district – 'Hampstead in Middlesex' – but is nevertheless showing signs of the future 'Hampstead in London'.

The first case recorded (1 May 1867) concerns a man who deserted from the army during the Crimean War, which is to say more than 10 years earlier: presumably he had only just been picked up. He agreed to go back and serve out his agreed term and 'the colonel is not desirous to prosecute'. Otherwise, the morning was chiefly devoted to some dirty piggeries in Well Lane, West End that were causing a nuisance; and also to an administrative scheme to connect a number of water closets in the district, which were currently fed by rainwater, to the mains pipes of the New River reservoir – the kind of preoccupation that would soon be taken out of the Justices' hands. On 6 May a woman living in Malden Road, Kentish Town (part of an estate laid out in houses during the previous 20 years) was brought to court by the police as having been found incapably drunk in Rosslyn Hill. Two days later three men appeared and were convicted of affray in a pub at Hendon; it was said, improbably, that there had been a drunken row over who had the smallest feet. Minutes do not always record the penalty imposed but in this case they do: 16/- each defendant, with an immediate alternative of 14 days in prison if the sums were not readily forthcoming. This was the usual practice, then and till well into the 20th century, but in the circumstances it seems a little hard. At the same sitting the Justices dealt with the theft of brandy from a cart, but the outcome of that case is not clear.

On 11 May two men from Flask Walk – today a smart address, but then a slummy little alley whose inhabitants rather often appeared in Court – were charged with stealing 'two live tame

ducks' from Lord Mansfield's property at Ken Wood. They had
been remanded in the police station cells for two days and were
now committed for trial at the Quarter Sessions in Clerkenwell,
presumably still in custody. At this period, in all magistrates' courts
cases of theft were treated with what we today would regard as
excessive severity, while cases involving violence tended to be viewed
more leniently than we would. Another inhabitant of Flask Walk,
convicted of stealing a cricket bat, stumps and pads, value 20/-,
was given 3 months' hard labour in the House of Correction (Cold
Bath Fields). Later the same month yet another inhabitant of Flask
Walk was in Court accused of assaulting a neighbour: the case was
dismissed on the dubious grounds that the complainant was
'cheeky' and 'saucy'.

Still in the same month a man was fined for driving cows on
the public highway in Hendon. He explained that he had been on
his way with them to Kentish Town. The number of open fields in
Kentish Town that could accommodate cows was fast dwindling:
possibly his destination was the Metropolitan Cattle Market on York
Way, immediately east of Kentish Town, which had been built in the
previous decade. In contrast to this cowherd from Hampstead's
rural past, at the Court's next sitting on 1 June there appeared the
first recorded example of a class of defendant later to become very
common in Hampstead – namely, men and women caught *in
flagrante delicto* on the Heath.

Obviously, from time immemorial, the inhabitants of the old
town must have been profiting from the relative privacy offered by
the Heath under cover of darkness. When I first began to come
across cases of prosecution for indecency, I was inclined to think it
rather hard on the young couples concerned – till a closer
examination of the evidence indicated that, in almost every case, the
police were pursuing prostitutes from outside the district who, with
the coming of cheap public transport, had begun to make use of the
fringes of the Heath as a convenient venue. In this first case, the
woman concerned (of whom the police constable remarked darkly
'I have seen her before') got away, leaving her client to bear the
embarrassment of being charged with 'indecently exposing his
person while having sexual intercourse'. The constable grudgingly
agreed that, since it was the early hours of Sunday morning, there
had been no other females near to be shocked by this sight, but
'ratepayers could have seen his person if any had been about.'

It was the ratepayers who paid for the police: therefore, the logic
went, they were the ones deserving of protection. Since the man had
already been in custody more than 24 hours when he appeared in
Court on Monday, he was let off with a caution.

Like their predecessors of a generation earlier, the Hampstead
Justices of the 1860s were still preoccupied with the unfortunate
and (for the ratepayers) expensive results of unregulated sexual
behaviour. Indeed, in the previous decade there had been a long-
running correspondence in the columns of *The Justice of the Peace* set
off by a letter which plaintively asked 'Why isn't fathering a bastard
a criminal offence?' (The common-sense explanation supplied by
the paper's lawyers did not satisfy all its readers.) It so happens that,
in this early summer of 1867, the case that took up most time and
resulted in page after page of scribbled notes, was of this kind. I
give the details here because they shed much incidental light on the
life-styles and class attitudes of the times. A teenage girl called Jane
Bland, of New End in Hampstead, had given birth the previous
October to 'a bastard child' (sex unspecified). She claimed that the
father was one John Gee Whittingstall Bean, who was probably not
fully grown himself, since she refers to him at one point in her
evidence as 'Master John'. She had been employed as a maid in
the Bean family home at Heath Mount, which I do not think can
have been the long-standing boys' school of that name but, rather,
another substantial house standing near the top of Heath Street.
At any rate, the Beans kept quite a large establishment:

> I left in July 1866. Connection took place on 15th January 1866.
> I am fairly sure it was on a Monday. . .No other servants in the
> house – only a boy servant. . .There was a fire in London that
> could be seen from my room and Mrs Beans', whilst I was gone
> downstairs to get some hot water he [John Bean] took the
> opportunity to get into my room. . .I am not on intimate terms
> with him he is not keeping company with me. . .It was at night,
> his mother was asleep in the parlour – no one else in the house he
> was with me about ten minutes. I went downstairs afterwards to
> get the place ready for the morning – he threatened me if I. . .'
> [*account illegible here*].

The next morning, John Bean apparently said to her 'If you
have given me anything I'll break your bl— neck.' Jane confided in

the visiting washerwoman while they were both at the tub: 'She said she knew there was something up. . .I started the conversation by saying that Master John had violated me. She said she suspected it from seeing me and knowing his character. I never had connection with him or anyone else before. . .His mother accused me. I had never been found fault with. They accused me of having the boy [servant boy] in the room. I made no complaint to my parents till I left.' She did not leave the Bean employment till July, 6 months pregnant, but she did, however, tell her elder sister earlier, in April, since at that point the sister called on Mrs Bean and a further scene took place, with John Bean present: ". . .His mother told him to tell the truth. She said 'Is it true that Jane is in the family way by you?' He said No at first. . .then said that it was the case but the child did not belong to him, he did not deny that he had had connection with me but that it did not belong to him. His mother died two days later."

That last, sudden statement, evocative of Victorian melodramas about errant sons breaking their mothers' hearts, was borne out in the sister's evidence. "Mrs Bean said 'How dare you come here to bring disgrace on my home?' [It is mentioned elsewhere that this sister had herself had a 'similar misfortune', i.e. an illegitimate pregnancy.] "Mrs Bean had a paralysis fit on the same evening from the shock and died two days afterwards." A note in the margin confirms the death, as if the JPs had independent knowledge of it. No doubt this abrupt disappearance of the mistress threw the household into some disarray, and this may have been the reason that, in spite of the confrontation, Jane continued to work there till her condition must have become apparent to everyone. Although Mr Bean senior was clearly still alive, since the house is referred to as his, he seems to have taken no part in these scenes, perhaps because he was conveniently away on business, or perhaps simply because pregnant servant girls did not normally fall within the province of the master of the house. "The defendant's brother Fred told me he could have given me medicine if he had know what had taken place. I sent my youngest sister about a fortnight before I was confined, with a note to the defendant. . ."

John Bean was represented in Court by a Mr Lewis, a solicitor who lived in a nearby house. It was claimed that he only occasionally resided at his father's house ('when ill') – that he had had to be 'summoned by Telegraph' for the traumatic interview in April – and

that he wasn't there at the earlier crucial time. Also 'I was suffering
from constitutional weakness at the period stated. . .I was under
Medical treatment'. A medical certificate to this effect was
apparently supplied, but the court, no doubt rightly wary of the
situation in which the professional classes appeared to be closing
ranks, did not regard it as good evidence. The defendant then
suggested rather lamely that 'the complainant came to his room to
put a mustard plaster on him'. . .'I did admit that I had connection
with you, but that I am not the father of the child."

Brother Fred contributed: 'I know nothing particular of the
complainant except that the boy [servant boy] was found there one
night. I was not present. I have seen her and the boy playing
together.'

The court does not seem to have been impressed by this further
attempt to deflect all the blame onto the working class. Significantly,
Mr Lewis did not call the servant boy as a witness, presumably
guessing that he would get nowhere with him and that further facts
damaging to John Bean might have come out instead.

An order was made against John Bean in the standard sum of
2/6 per week, plus 15/- for the doctor and 10/- for the nurse as the
cost of Jane Bland's confinement. Mr Lewis announced that his
client would appeal, but I doubt if he did. The allegation by Jane
Bland that he had violated her was not explored.

The Bland–Bean case was exceptional in that a middle-class
family figured in it. Today, anyone from any background may find
him or herself in a magistrates' court on a motoring offence, but the
19th-century court catered almost exclusively for the working classes
– hence the 'voyage into unknown London' tone adopted by some
journalists. The feeling that comes from the Hampstead records of
the time is that Marshall, Read and their colleagues, ever mindful no
doubt of the undisciplined hordes down the hill who might threaten
the peace of Hampstead, felt it their duty to 'come down hard' on
troublesome behaviour, even in first offenders – or particularly on
first offenders, who might be reformed by being taught a lesson. An
unspoken agenda of 'saving' people, carried over from the prevailing
religious convictions of the time, seems to permeate the Court's
decisions.

This is particularly marked in the case of juveniles, who were
still dealt with in the adult courts. Thus, in July 1868 we find a boy
of eleven who had been caught stealing gooseberries and cherries

valued at twopence, in company with another who had got away, was
sent to the House of Correction for seven days and ordered six
strokes of the birch. This apparently harsh disposal is at variance
with the much gentler treatment meted out to another small boy
caught stealing pears from a tree later in the month: he was kept in
custody for the night but then discharged with a caution. Perhaps
this latter boy looked very small and sorry, whereas the other may
have been a known local nuisance already. The fact that the parents
'demanded that he might be sent to an Industrial school' would
suggest a number of previous offences, for the Industrial school
system (founded in the mid-century as the first step towards
removing youngsters from adult prisons) was a well-intentioned if
draconian method of taking boys away altogether from the world of
the streets.

During the same month, a boy of fourteen who had stolen a
flannel petticoat and blanket in Friern Barnet was held in custody
for five days, then brought back to Court and given a further week
with hard labour and 'a whipping'. Present perceptions of justice
would regard it as inequitable that juveniles were subjected to
corporal punishment in addition to prison for trivial offences when
adult males were not, but in fairness it has to be said that the
magistrates were only treating these working-class boys in the way
their own sons were routinely treated at public schools.

The blanket and the flannel petticoat were most probably stolen
from a washing line for re-sale: such thefts were commonplace in
those days when absolute poverty was a reality. They bear out the
view that most 19th-century crimes were not in fact carried out by
criminals, but were more often opportunist, impulsive and
sometimes very stupid. In the same session, one labourer was
convicted of stealing a trowel, combs, a tobacco box, a pencil and
two handkerchiefs from another. He said he had 'borrowed' them
but then had sold them. That earned him 3 weeks' hard labour. A
servant girl, working in one of the rather grand modern houses in
Belsize Park Gardens, stole '1 table cloth and other articles to value,
15s.' The lady of the house stated she had 'found the things in her
box. She said her fellow servant had put them there... most of the
articles are marked in my name.' The policeman in the case 'had a
chat with her. She has only been a month from Ireland.' Probably
little more than a child and certainly quite unequipped for life in
London, she was dispatched for three months' hard labour. Living-

in servants, most of them female, formed a huge class of their own in mid-Victorian London, and one sees that the offence of stealing from an employer would have to be regarded seriously or the whole situation would have become unmanageable. However, her fate contrasts with that of a Hampstead man who, accused the same month for 'threatening to shoot his wife. . .to blow her brains out' was simply bound over to keep the peace.

One of the sketchiest cases revealed in the minute book for that year appears in a different, more clerkly hand. In December a labourer was charged with having been found 'in the enclosed premises of Burrough's Farm, Hendon, supposed for some unlawful purpose and not giving a satisfactory account of himself.' A police constable on night duty out there 'heard a gentleman's dog barking. . . Saw the prisoner and two other men coming up the field – they saw me and ran away and I pursued and caught him, they must have got through the Hedge to get into the field, and no footpath. I asked him what he was doing there and he said he was coming to find a place to lay down – he said he did not know the other men – he was not drunk – it was moonlight – his boots and trowsers were very wet and dirty – he did not say that he had lost his way.' This evidence was corroborated only by another officer who 'had been told that 3 suspicious looking men were seen. . .coming through the fence.' On this vague, hearsay basis, the man was given 14 days' hard labour. One can only suppose that the magistrates were quite convinced that a planned burglary had been intercepted and did not scruple about the quality of the evidence, though it could also be said that if the man's story was true, taking an apparently homeless man into a fortnight's custody in the middle of winter could be seen as an act of charity.

By the time the 1870s are reached the impression is of quite a large, shifting population of the homeless, mainly male, many of them from distant parts of the country, passing through the workhouse at New End. After 1868, with the change in the administration and the introduction of casual wards, the long preoccupation with sending paupers back to their own parishes was at an end. The Justices no longer sat regularly in the workhouse, but the minute books show that occasional court sessions were still held there when the business of the morning was the misbehaviour of the inmates. The usual charges (apart from drunkenness) were that a defendant had refused to do the work allotted to him in return for his night's lodging in the casual ward, or, more obscurely, that he had 'destroyed his clothes'. The frequency of this charge makes it clear that men, and occasionally women, had understood very well that if they rendered their own dirty and threadbare clothes unwearable the Poor Law Guardians would feel obliged to supply them with better ones. The days were gone when the poor were suffered to wander round in rags and half naked. For decency's sake as well as charity the destitute must be adequately clad, though naturally the Guardians were infuriated when the clothes supplied were then pawned or sold.

The usual sentence for these workhouse offences was a week in prison with hard labour, and the same penalty, in the 1870s, was handed out to beggars, for begging was no longer tolerated as a fact of life in the way it had been a generation earlier. An awareness spread round society that asking for money must at least be disguised as offering to sell matches or penny toys, sweep streets or carry luggage – an understanding that only came unravelled a century later under the Conservative administration of the 1980s. The case of a man going from house to house in South Hill Park in February 1880 indicates the view by then taken by both the police and the respectable working classes such as railway employees: it also, incidentally, provides a snapshot view of one of the new areas of Hampstead just taking shape:

> PC's evidence: 'When he saw me he ran away across the brickfield to the railway line, 3 platelayers stopped him, I asked him why he ran away from me and he said 'You know'. I said what, and he said 'Begging'.'

Drink cases also begin to figure frequently at this period, and involved women almost as often as men. Whether people were really drinking more or whether society was now less tolerant is a moot point. The charge with a female defendant was often 'drunk and incapable of taking care of herself', a wording suggesting a social concern for the women's welfare which may or may not have been borne out in practice. In any event, the penalty was usually a short spell in custody. Clearly, the chances of any member of the disreputable poor being able to pay even a small fine on the spot at that date were low, but inevitably this led to the working classes going to prison for offences that would not attract the same penalty at a different level of society. When, in October 1876, two defendants given as 'gentlemen', residing near Regent's Park, were convicted of 'wilfully extinguishing the lamps in Loudon [sic] Road' they escaped with a fine of 30/- each plus costs, and the question of whether or not they had been drunk at the time was not examined.

Several offences brought to court in these years seem so trivial that one feels that the steadily evolving society was actually looking for things to prosecute. In addition to the trickle of boys stealing fruit from orchards, two 10-year-olds from Kentish Town were brought up in July 1874 for 'wilfully damaging a number of works at Lower Park Road'. This was an extensive building site at the time, and local children were apparently using it as an adventure playground. The two boys in question were 'discharged. . .on the parents' promising to punish them and prevent the mischief in future' when a carpenter gave evidence that these were only two among 'about a hundred boys' who had been involved – an insight into the number of unoccupied children roaming the London streets unsupervised once the new Board Schools were shut for the summer. Another case concerned teenage boys found throwing 'missiles' at passers-by, which turned out to be orange peel. This case, like a few others, is noted on separate pages pinned into the book afterwards, which suggests that the boys were carried off there and then to one of the JPs, who had heard the matter in his own house as in past days.

More officious seems a Metropolitan Board of Works summons in October 1882 of a man for playing cricket on the Heath, which was dismissed because 'the Bench considered that the defendant had established a bona fide claim of right.' Behind this anodyne remark lies an on-going tension: the Heath had in principle been secured for use by the public in perpetuity in 1871, but there were then anxieties for decades that the Board of Works, and then the LCC, might try to turn it from a natural-looking heath into more tightly controlled parkland. Further investigation reveals that the cricket game in question was deliberately staged, in the full knowledge that the MBW would prosecute. The participants had assembled a mass of evidence as to their right to play on the Heath; in addition, the men who sat on the Bench were the very same or moved in the same circles as those who had fought to keep the Heath unbuilt on. The most frequently sitting Justices in the 1880s were Joseph Hoare; Basil Woodd Smith, who lived for many years at Branch Hill Lodge, a historic house at the top of Frognal; and Major-General Agnew from Belsize Park Gardens. Another energetic and long-serving magistrate was John Samuel Fletcher, who later became Hampstead's MP. He lived in various houses near the 'New Road' – Finchley Road, which, till near the end of the century, ran north of Swiss Cottage through mainly open fields.

The Summary Jurisdiction Act of 1879 had specified for the first time just how the court record should be kept. It is therefore from January 1880 that we find proper registers for Hampstead, which show less detail than the minute books but cover the full range of cases, including all the uncontested ones where often no notes were made. The Heath is a constant presence in them. On 27 March 1880 we hear of pickpockets at the Easter Fair and of men there fined for 'gambling with ha'pence – with sticks and rings' (fine 2/6). Others that year and the following ones were fined for cutting up the turf on the Heath by riding or drawing carts across it, for damaging trees, throwing stones, and grazing animals illicitly there. One man turned two apes out onto the Heath (fine 7/6) and did it again at the same time the following year, others plied donkeys for hire in the wrong part of the Heath. Donkey rides had by then become a traditional part of a Sunday excursion to the Heath; the earliest case in the Hampstead records of cruelty to an animal dates from 1874, when a donkey driver was charged with 'ill-treating three asses by beating them continually with sticks in East Heath Road.' Each donkey was carrying someone and they were going up a steep hill. A police constable had been called by 'a concerned person'. The constable stated that the driver had told him 'that he was aware it was cruel but they were young donkeys fresh from Ireland and it was necessary to beat them to break them in. I took him into custody.' (Fine 20/- or 14 days. The fine was paid).

An indecent exposure case in February 1883, which was not this time associated with any heterosexual activity, suggests that some activities on the Heath never change, while a sadder case evokes a rather older world: a woman called Eliza Hill was charged with 'abandoning and exposing an infant whereby its health was endangered.' The baby was found dead on the Heath, and evidence revealed a pathetic saga of the mother trying to persuade a neighbour to nurse it and the neighbour getting it some 'food'. The constable who found it, with an empty feeding bottle by its side, 'thought it about a week old – a miserable looking child'. The workhouse doctor who examined it was of the opinion that it had died of starvation. Pinned into the book at this point is a sheet of paper with the rules of the Workhouse Home for Fallen Women in Kilburn and on the other side, a note that the defendant had been admitted to the home earlier in the summer, having been confined in Queen Charlotte's Hospital, but had left almost immediately. The case was remanded till the following week, but the surviving records do not reveal the outcome.

It is worth recording that the coroner for Central Middlesex in the mid-Victorian period, an energetic and forthright person called Edwin Lankester, expressed the view that the dead infants actually found in the rapidly expanding London of the time were only a small fraction of the total, many more being successfully concealed by their desperate mothers.

6 In sight of the 20th century

Before me as I write is a large silver inkstand with a tiny glass ink-
container at its centre and a lid to cover it, with a substantial dent
in it that suggests it was once used as a missile. Round its base is
a worn inscription saying that it belonged to Henry Clarke DL JP,
chairman of the Hampstead Bench from 1897 to 1914, and that in
the 1920s it was presented to the magistrates in his memory by his
son, Percy Clarke. The handsome courthouse (p 49) that opened in
Hampstead at about the time Henry Clarke's long spell as chairman
came to an end has itself come to its end as a courthouse, which is
why the inkstand now serves me as a somewhat cumbersome
paperweight.

I assume that Henry Clarke, who bought Cannon Hall from
James Marshall JP in the early 1880s, was a Justice on Hampstead
Bench before he became chairman, but because of the lack of proper
records of Hampstead's magistrates after 1894 it is difficult to trace
his full career. The same is true of others towards the end of the
century and in the early years of the new one, but Basil Woodd
Smith (p 58) was still active through the 1890s and was, I think,
chairman before Clarke. Another prominent Justice of the period
was Edward Gotto, an internationally successful drainage engineer
at a time when main drainage had become the touchstone of
civilisation. As a young man he had had extensive experience in
north London with the embryo metropolitan authority, but he later
worked as far afield as Rio de Janeiro. On the proceeds he built
himself, next to the Heath on land that had earlier formed part
of the Cannon Hall estate, a large house, eclectic in style,
inappropriately called The Logs and described by Pevsner as
mixing Italianate, Gothic and French styles in extravagant abandon.

Other long-serving JPs of the period were a Dr Weaver, a
Major-General Young and a couple of Colonels. In general, there
do not seem to have been more than half a dozen fully active
Hampstead Justices at any one time, though there were usually
a few more who were too grand or too busy to sit regularly. It was
still the practice, then and for the early decades of the 20th century,
for the status of JP to be conferred as an honour on a citizen who
was prominent for other reasons – Mayor (for example Sir Henry
Harben, first mayor of the Metropolitan Borough of Hampstead

created in 1900), member of the LCC or of the House of Lords: the appointment did not necessarily imply any duties to be undertaken. This was especially so in the London area where for much of the 19th century the Middlesex Justices had little to do. A letter of 1886 addressed to the Clerk of the Peace at Middlesex Sessions House on Clerkenwell Green, from someone who had evidently been helping to revise the record, concludes 'There are many names on your list that I have never heard of before as acting in my division, and they certainly never attend any of the meetings.'

Of the grander Hampstead worthies, Samuel Hoare JP, grandson of the magistrate of the 1820s, was by the 1890s living in London's West End and therefore sitting in the Hanover Square division. Heath House, his grandfather's residence, was now occupied by Lord Glenesk JP, who had another address in Piccadilly: he does not figure in the Hampstead registers. But it is clear that a few committed Hampstead Justices were prepared to sit consistently at the regular Petty Sessions, even when these began to take place more than once a week. Sometimes, indeed, four or more sat together (today, three is the norm) and it had become rare for one to sit on his own. Major-General Young did hold one session alone soon after Easter in April 1895 because all his colleagues were 'ill or away' but the comment in the *Hampstead Express* was 'fortunately the business was very light'.

Business continued light in Hampstead, in spite of the all the new houses now filling up West Hampstead and the Gospel Oak area. In fact, the transformation of Hampstead from the centre of a large rural district to a more concentrated urban area had the effect of reducing, slightly, the numbers of charges heard. Even the crowded urban district of Kentish Town to the south was basically too respectable to produce much succulent crime – apart from a celebrated murder in 1890 involving a mother, a baby and a jealous lady-friend – though serious, urgent cases were now sometimes taken before the stipendiary magistrates at Marylebone Court, who attended every day. Three months before Major-General Young's single-handed session, the same *Hampstead Express* newspaper reporter, recounting routine summonses for misbehaviour in the workhouse Casual Ward, added 'The only other cases at this court throughout the week have been one or two charges of drunkenness.'

With the increase in houses and population came a lavish increase in the numbers of police to patrol the area: 83 men were

stationed at Hampstead in 1877, according to the usually reliable
F E Baines, and only 7 years later there were 150. If this was a
preventive measure against a feared crime-wave it seems to have
been most effective; one has the impression that, as the century
neared its end, the police went out actively looking for miscreants.
They were enjoined to prowl the streets at night, trying doors and
windows to make sure they were locked and acting as a reassuring –
or intimidating – presence for any stray, late pedestrian. Domestic
burglary was a rare occurrence anyway, since the poor had little worth
stealing and the rich always had servants in their houses whether they
themselves were at home or not. When a case of breaking and entering
a dwelling house did occur, as it did in January 1896 when £70 worth
of plate and jewellery were stolen in Hampstead, the magistrates sent
the offender straight to the Old Bailey.

The following month, for good measure, they sentenced to 21
days' hard labour a 'suspected person' under an old Act relating to
Rogues and Vagabonds, but a large proportion of the charges that
occupied their time were matters that would not have been brought
to court a few years earlier: failing to muzzle a dog, or to send a
child to school or to get him or her vaccinated.

In the last decade of the century registers began to be kept in
standard-issue ledgers headed 'Register of the Court of Summary
Jurisdiction sitting at…'. They were properly signed now by each
magistrate in attendance and in other respects looked more like the
registers of the present day, except that no dates of birth or ages
were yet given for adults. Nor, contrary to modern practice, was
it usually noted where the offence was committed – except for the
frequent mentions of Hampstead Heath, where indecency of various
kinds continued to be popular, or at any rate fervently combated
by the now copious police force. (£2 a head was the most usual fine
at this date, though sometimes, if the woman was not known to the
police, she got off with a smaller fine than her partner, presumably
on the grounds that he might have led her on.) Such charges, and
others for lighting illicit fires on the Heath, drunk and disorderly
behaviour, assault and gambling, peaked sharply at certain dates
in April or May, which must have been those of the Easter and
Whitsun Fairs. These had become major events in the Cockney
calendar, attracting up to 100,000 people and confirming the
Heath's status as a general London playground.

At more peaceful times of the year the police had the leisure to prosecute Heath users for picking wild flowers, stealing earth, and for 'furiously riding bicycles' – June 1895, fine 10/- a head. Ten shillings was a weekly wage to a substantial proportion of Londoners, and 'round about a pound a week' was an ordinary working-class family income. Police constables themselves started their career on only 24/- a week, which may explain how London could afford so many of them, at a time when bank clerks got about three times as much, and the professional classes £700 a year and upwards – sometimes, in the grander Hampstead homes, up to many thousands. The relatively high fine imposed on the cyclists must have reflected their perceived middle-class status.

The Heath also had its darker side. In 1895, as in other years, a young woman attempted to commit suicide in one of its ponds. Suicide was technically a felony and would remain so till 1961; in earlier times failed suicides had been harshly treated, even to the application of the death penalty – a punishment which could have had no value as a deterrent. In the mid-19th century attempted suicides had been sentenced to hard labour. But the girl who tried to drown herself in August 1895 was 'discharged with caution, order made for detention not exceeding 14 days in the Workhouse infirmary as an alleged lunatic' – a type of disposal which had by then become standard as a way round the letter of the law.

Hampstead, like all courts, had its more diverting moments. In the same spring (1895) that the local paper journalist commented on the lack of much going on, a north London clergyman called the Rev W J Jenkins was a frequent attender. He appeared on 30 March contesting a summons for assault and abusive oaths and attempting to cross-charge another with the same offences. There had been an altercation between the two men in a railway carriage waiting at Muswell Hill station as to whether a window should be open or not, and insults such as 'downright cad', 'no gentleman' and 'blackguard' had been traded, but there seems to have been a previous history between them of neighbourhood dispute over a fence. It is clear that Jenkins was already a familiar figure in the court, for when he entered the witness box the presiding justice, a Mr Bodkin sitting with three others, said 'Now, Mr Jenkins, what's the form of oath today?' (*Laughter*). 'The reverend gentleman claimed to be sworn in the Scotch form and insisted that the Chairman of the Bench must stand up, and with uplifted hands administer the oath. Mr Bodkin declined to do this.'

He was eventually found guilty and charged 20/- plus costs. A fortnight later he was back again, this time wanting a summons against a coalman for refusing to weigh sacks from which coal had just been shot into his coal cellar. Evidence was submitted that he had tried to make the same application the previous week and had been told by the Justices' Clerk, Frank Beal, that he couldn't. The magistrates also took the view that 'no offence had been committed which would justify them in granting a summons'. Jenkins then tried to read a further statement aloud and was told he couldn't 'but Lord Chief Justice Campbell said that I must indict the Bench' – etc.

On 20 April, under the heading 'Mr Jenkins again' the *Hampstead Express* reported that this persistent customer had appeared once more, this time at the North London Police Court which had been opened in Dalston in 1889 to take some of the expanding workload from other courts north of the Thames, including Clerkenwell. This time he wanted a summons against certain railway officials for being rude to him and detaining him when, in company with his wife, he refused to show them his tickets. This summons too was refused, and there followed more protests and the citing again of high legal authority.

In private life, a Justice might feel sorry for a would-be respectable citizen so clearly in the grip of some persecution complex, but the exasperating, tedious and occasionally painful nature of court work inevitably make magistrates welcome the Jenkinses of this world as light relief. I have cited this case not so much for its period features, though vicars and railway carriages were both staples of Victorian jokes, as for its modern ring. The time when magistrates were almost automatically high-handed with those who came before them in any capacity was past. Mr Jenkins was allowed to have his days in court, to have his say within reason, and was treated with at least a veneer of politeness. Evidence was taken with more care and attention to detail than it had been in earlier decades, and magistrates knew that they were servants of the Law, not its masters. Essentially, the 20th-century magistrates' court had arrived.

Jenkins himself was not represented by a lawyer (Jenkinses in any era, including the present day, find it difficult to get a lawyer to represent them for long). However, from about this time defence lawyers appeared more often in court, though no legal aid came in till 1903 and would not be extended in any form to the magistrates' courts until 1930. But by the 1890s fewer convicted defendants found themselves at once on their way to prison; fines as an alternative to custody were becoming more frequent. For instance, in September 1901, a servant girl who pleaded guilty to stealing two gold brooches, value £3.12.0, from her master's shop in Hampstead High Street, was said to be otherwise 'of good character'. In the not very distant past, such a deed would have attracted an immediate sentence of hard labour, but this girl escaped with a fine of £5, with one month in gaol as an alternative. (Since 1879 the tariff for custody in lieu of payment had been fixed by statute.) A note in the register adds 'Prisoner's aunt attended and paid fine'.

Around 1900, magistrates were still ordering beatings for small boys caught stealing fruit or throwing stones, but there are signs that a greater awareness of child offenders as a special group was emerging: they were no longer sent to adult gaols. Court sessions for juveniles only did not officially come into being until after the Children Act of 1908, but already in Hampstead in the mid-1890s it appears to have been customary to group together cases involving children and hear them in one sitting. At such a sitting in October 1896 a 12-year-old who had stolen a parcel from a van containing two petticoats, value 7/6, and an 11-year-old who had stolen a pair of spectacles, value 2/-, were both sent to Feltham Industrial School till the age of 16; but it should at once be said that this was then regarded, at any rate by the magisterial class, as a humane disposal in that it provided an education and a fresh start. Not all Industrial Schools, in any case, were exclusively for those with criminal convictions. The one in Regent's Park Road also admitted boys in need of care; this was probably the destination of the 11-year-old who, the same year, was found in Hampstead 'wandering and destitute'. With similar overall intent, no doubt, shortly before Christmas 1901, two brothers aged 14 and 15 charged with stealing money from the landlady were committed to a Reformatory boarding school in Ware 'till the age of nineteen'. Evidently it was hoped they would take advantage of the opportunity to turn over a new leaf, since it was noted approvingly 'both lads Church of England'. The time was still 20 years' distant when the metropolitan magistrate Geoffrey Rose would question publicly whether it was sensible or even moral to send working-class offenders away 'from home, parents, brothers and sisters, possibly good, to live in a collection of delinquents at a public institution for months or years' (an address to the Magistrates' Association in 1923).

Court registers inevitably reflect, at first in a tentative and inconspicuous way, far-reaching changes in material conditions of life and social customs, which is why they are more interesting 100 years on than in their own time. For example, in December 1898, there appears a summons, at the request of the Hampstead Vestry that was soon to become the Borough Council, for the amount due for the supply of electric light to a household. It must have been a large house or the bill must have been outstanding a long time, for it came to the considerable sum of £14.1.1, plus costs. In July 1901, a defendant living in West Hampstead was similarly summoned, for a bill of £6.15.4. 'Town Clerk stated that defendant had sent a cheque for that amount and that he would like the summons adjourned for seven days'. So 'Cheque – seven days to clear', a mantra so often pronounced in courts today, when almost no fines are paid in full on the spot, was then just beginning to modify the courts' traditional demand for immediate cash. In theory a defendant with a fixed address in the area had been able to ask for 'time to pay' since 1879, but this does not seem to have become the general practice till after the World War I. Till then, a defendant who had been sentenced in his absence would not even necessarily know about the fine till a policeman appeared on his doorstep to take him off to prison for non-payment.

Another sign of the times in the early 1900s is the large number of prosecutions for cruelty to horses, usually by driving them when they were not in a fit state or when the cart or van was overloaded. Often the evidence suggests that the drivers, who were usually the horse's owners as well, were motivated less by brutality than by the need to earn a living in the only way they could, but some of the evidence makes harrowing reading and, certainly by 1910, the court almost never dismissed a case. The usual penalty was a fine, plus the police vet's fee for examining and advising on the animal, plus costs, and sometimes the horse was ordered to be destroyed. It would be unrealistic to suppose that this form of cruelty was actually on the increase in the 1890s and the 1900s; it seems clear that what had increased was public sensitivity to the matter. This was by no means confined to Hampstead: in Clerkenwell too such prosecutions were quite frequent, though there they were almost always initiated by one or other of the local police constables who made it their business to keep an eye on horseflesh. The right-thinking middle

classes of Hampstead were particularly aware of animal welfare:
Hampstead had its own Society for the Protection of Animals, and
an Anti-Bearing Association (opposed to the use of the bearing rein
to hold horse's heads high in elegant discomfort) had been formed
there in the 1890s. The Association was responsible for placing near
the foot of Hampstead's steepest main ascent, a white sign painted
in elegant black script saying 'Please slacken bearing rein going up
the hill'. It was still there in the late 1950s, long after horse-drawn
traffic had been reduced to the occasional brewer's dray.

It is one of the ironies of the law that it often exerts itself to deal
with an age-old problem just when the problem is being overtaken
by a new one. In the late 1920s, a Hampstead Justice was to remark
that, thankfully, with the change from horse to motor traffic, cruelty
cases had become rare. In the very same sitting in May 1912 at
which Henry Clarke and his colleagues dealt with several cases of
ill-treated horses, they also convicted several motorists for exceeding
the (very low) speed restriction, for being drunk, for failing to stop
when requested, for having no licence plates or lights, or for
'travelling backwards with a motor car inconveniently for occupants
and traffic'. The car, which was to dominate and clog the work of
magistrates' courts later in the century, eventually accounting for
over half the cases heard, was fast arriving.

What was happening in Clerkenwell this long time? The Court
there, sitting every day with two resident stipendiary magistrates
turn by turn, remained far busier than Hampstead. The area that
had always been Clerkenwell, now divided between the LCC
boroughs of Holborn, Finsbury, St Pancras and Islington, stayed
extremely crowded and predominantly poor. Some of the business
from Islington that it had previously handled was now hived off to
other courts, such as the North London, but there was still more
than enough daily business to fill Clerkenwell's one court room,
particularly since its district included the now heavily built-up area
north of the Euston Road, behind the big railway stations. Plans
were laid, and in the late November of 1900 an editorial in *The
Builder* stated with satisfaction: 'It is well known that the London
police courts are quite inadequate in both their number and the
accommodation they provide to meet the increasing requirements
of the Metropolis. . .It is announced that a new police-court is about
to be built in Shoreditch, with two courtrooms, to replace that in

Worship-Street; another at Clerkenwell, adjoining the present one; one in Tooley-street, with two courts and a police-station, near the Tower Bridge south approach; and one for Westminster. . .Mr Dixon Butler is, we believe, the Official Architect to the Receiver for the Metropolitan [Police] District...'

Dixon Butler was indeed responsible for a large number of London courts. Hampstead, which seems to take a leaf or two out of Lutyens' book, was one of his later ones. Clerkenwell (p 36) was described by Walter Besant, writing in 1911 for the earliest Survey of London volumes, as 'built of red brick and Bath stone in a clean, pleasant style, usually associated with public libraries' (see also Pevsner's comment, p 37). Its construction removed the old courtroom with, apparently, all the existing register and minute books, which is why there has been nothing to quote from Clerkenwell before 1905, when at last a series of surviving books begins.

The district of Clerkenwell had changed somewhat since the middle of the 19th century. The mass of small trades centred round Clerkenwell Green, including gold-beating, watch-making and lock-making, still survived. Exmouth Market flourished. In many parts of Clerkenwell many old houses remained which had turned into slums (*see below*). But Clerkenwell Road and Rosebery Avenue had been built, lined with tall blocks, cutting a swathe of prosaic Victorian modernity through former twisting lanes and alleys; and dull, wide

SLUMS OF "LITTLE ITALY" INSPECTED BY THE CLERKENWELL MAGISTRATE YESTERDAY.

Farringdon Road, with a railway line running alongside, now covered the lower course of the Fleet ditch. A number of ancient corners that had come to be considered particularly slummy, such as Peartree Court and Turnmill Street, had been rebuilt with Model Workmen's Dwellings.

But rebuilding an area does not transform its inhabitants, and the people of Clerkenwell had not changed much since the days when Angus B Reach had described its 'squalid courts' and 'dens' in vivid prose. Superficially, changes had taken place. If there was rather less 'grovelling, starveling poverty' by the 1900s it was because England enjoyed a much greater general prosperity than in the 1840s, and because there had grown up a whole social infrastructure, both charitable and controlling. Board Schools, hospitals, orphanages, reform schools, out-relief for destitute families, Church Missions, inspectors for this and that, the police force and the courts themselves, all exerted a coercive influence on the more anarchic sections of society. For a member of the middle classes to make his way through the streets of Clerkenwell could no longer be considered a descent into a dangerous jungle, even in the overwrought mind of a Reach – in any case the worst dangers had moved eastwards, to the Whitechapel of the Ripper murders and the Limehouse of reputed opium dens. Artful Dodgers no longer roamed in gangs and it was generally agreed that most London streets were wonderfully respectable and safe compared with 60 or even 40 years before – 'blackguardism and ruffianly behaviour are today seldom seen,' as *The Times* put it. In addition, although so many more activities were now illegal, crime rates had been falling since the early 1880s. (They rose again slightly around 1908, then continued to fall up to and during World War I. A significant rise only began in the 1920s.)

In spite of all this apparent improvement, suggesting that the Victorians' faith in the progress of mankind was amply justified, enough citizens of Clerkenwell continued to misbehave to keep the court occupied. Thanks to the acumen of the Chief Clerk of the 1990s, who rescued some sheets of paper from behind a desk drawer, there exist 'Comparative Returns of Work' for Clerkenwell Police Court for most of the years 1896 to 1917. These gross up various figures, including totals, types of disposal and overall charges for the year. The overall figures run from 9726 people charged in 1896 to 8228 in 1917, with the figure in intervening

years occasionally nudging over 10,000 and twice (1898 and '99)
over 11,000, but with the general trend, in conformity with national
rates, slightly downwards.

However, all things are relative. As one turns the pages of the
actual registers of the court, once these became available, a picture
emerges of an irrepressibly lively and wayward community contained
more or less on the right side of the law by the constant exertions
of a large number of equally lively and robust police officers. Cecil
M Chapman, who was briefly a stipendiary at Clerkenwell at the
turn of the century and who wrote his memoirs a quarter of a
century later, evokes just this situation:

> I cannot refrain from telling how one day at Clerkenwell I was
> confronted by what appeared to be a well-dressed lady wearing
> a smart straw hat, and I looked at my list to see what she was
> accused of. To my astonishment I found the name of a man
> charged with masquerading in women's clothes for an illegal
> purpose. I could not help smiling when I heard an excellent
> detective describe how he had met the prisoner and being
> suspicious said to him "I believe you are a man", whereupon
> the prisoner struck him in the eye, saying, "I am a woman, you
> fool; take that," and then closed with him, and they both rolled
> upon what the detective called the floor until the prisoner was
> overpowered.

7 Keeping the peace in Clerkenwell

During the 1990s the traditional minor charge of 'drunk and disorderly' largely disappeared from the lists of London courts. Public drunkenness, frequently associated with street drinking, has become tolerated *faute de mieux* by an over-stretched police force with its mind on other things; when the disorderliness reaches an exaggerated stage the police today tend to arrest, caution and release the drunk later, rather than go through the laborious paperwork now required to bring any individual to court. For more than 100 years, however, 'Dr/dis' was one of commonest charges laid: in the early 1900s almost half of those taken into custody in this metropolitan district were allegedly drunk and frequently disorderly too, or some other variant such as using obscene language, urinating in public, 'insulting behaviour', 'annoying passers-by' or obstructing the officer in the course of his duty. Five shillings or one day was the standard penalty, though this could rise steeply for habitual offenders.
A Toynbee Trust investigation of the period found that roughly a quarter of those charged as drunk were women, a notably high figure, since women drunk enough to be taken into custody have been something of a rarity in more recent times. But the early registers of Clerkenwell, complemented by the minute books, bear the statistic out.

Drink was no doubt a contributory factor in other cases, particularly in quarrels and assaults between neighbours or couples. As the journalist working for the Toynbee Trust put it: 'There is always a constant demand for summonses for assault, and a large proportion of these are issued by wives against husbands.' Public houses were open all day – the idea of licensing hours, which later became such a feature of British life and shaped the concept of 'respectable' drinking for several generations, was brought in under the Defence of the Realm Act in World War I in an effort to keep well-paid munitions workers sober. In spite of strenuous efforts by the Temperance Society, working-class culture was largely a drinking culture. Late-Victorian and Edwardian London contained an enormous number of pubs, welcoming, spacious places, glittering with gaslight and cut glass, much more obviously attractive than the usual one- or two-room home in a multi-occupied house full of children and wet washing. On the delayed return from the pub, the resentments and tensions generated on all sides by such a life readily came to the surface.

The case of Thomas Powell, a labourer, is typical of many others. On 3 July 1905, he was fined 20/- plus 20/- costs, for assaulting his daughter – he threw a china cup at her. The police constable who was called to the scene testified that she had sustained 'a nasty cut'. The daughter stated 'Father had had a drop, [*to the father in the dock*] I said before you threw it, you wouldn't do it if my young man was there.' Other similar cases that year, which quite often involved a woman attacking a man as well as vice versa, mentioned sticks, jugs, basins, lamps and glass ornaments as ready-to-hand weapons, and a monotonous litany of 'He/she came back from the public house'. There is, however, a more timeless quality to the case of Hannah Shay, a laundress of 35, who was charged on 5 July with wilfully damaging four panes of glass, value 6/9. It happened about 10:30 at night and the principal witness – apparently the owner of the house, on the fringe of Islington – stated 'Prisoner came and asked me to wake my lodger up, I refused, she broke panes of glass'. A slightly different aspect to the story appears in what the prisoner said to the police when arrested: 'Serve her right. She shouldn't keep my husband there.'

This case, in common with many others at this date, reached the courts by way of a private summons taken out by the aggrieved party: the procedure cost 2/-, but the fee was sometimes waived 'in needy cases'. The time when the police would more or less automatically take over prosecution for assault or criminal damage still lay in the future. But when the offence erupted in public, the police did not hesitate to intervene. Partly because of the lack of space at home, domestic rows often took place in the street, a spectacle much enjoyed by passers-by, who would gather round to watch: that, of course, enabled the police to arrest the wrangling parties for breaching the peace. The commonly used phrase in police evidence, as reported in the minutes, is 'So I took him': 'I took her for bad language. . .I said, I'm taking you for indecency. . .I closed with him, threw him and took him.' Quite often the police got hit too, and paraded their bruised shins or cut lips indignantly before the magistrate, but it is clear that, not having to fear knives or guns (which are *never* mentioned at this period), they were very willing to have a go. Although the defendant often went to prison, there was usually the alternative of a fine; one has the impression that assaulting an officer of the law was not regarded as seriously then as it is today. Constables were themselves not immune to the effects of alcohol: it was a recognised problem, for they routinely accepted drinks in public houses, perhaps for turning a blind eye here and there. No doubt this was why, when more stringent licensing laws were brought in during World War I, serving alcohol to a policeman in uniform was made an offence.

Little larceny was reported in Edwardian Clerkenwell, partly, no doubt, because there were so many people out and about at most hours who would see it happening and raise the alarm. The most typical theft was of something like brass or iron or lead piping, or coals from a warehouse, often committed by a carter. A few people were charged with receiving stolen goods, usually linen or trinkets taken by dishonest servants from the more respectable streets of the Lloyd Baker estate near the court itself. In what was presumably a similar case, a 14-year-old was charged with giving a false name and address when offering a pledge in a pawnshop. The small amount of pilfering from shops often involved pathetically trivial items reflecting everyday need, such as a pair of boots, a bottle of cough mixture or a button hook. The very few more serious thefts – enterprising pickpocketing, for instance, in Exmouth Market, or clocks from a jewellers – were remanded at once to the Quarter Sessions.

In the late autumn of 1905 a solitary case appears that does sound like an attempt at house burglary, but may have reflected a situation nearer to French farce. Henry Jones, aged 21, was charged with being 'a suspected man in a bedroom'. He had been found in the evening in a house in Seymour Street (present-day Eversholt Street) by the householder, a railway carriage cleaner. Jones was behind the door of the first-floor back bedroom, with no boots on. The householder shouted for his wife who, perhaps fortunately for her, was elsewhere in the house at the time. Jones then 'said he had made a mistake and that his friends lived in Johnson Street' (Cranleigh Street, at right-angles). His boots were indeed on the downstairs doormat, though whether he had taken them off so as not to be heard or simply so as not to get mud on his supposed friends' floor was anyone's guess. He was remanded in custody for 2 days but then discharged for lack of evidence. What strikes one nowadays is the way no one was surprised that Jones was able just to walk in. Front doors then stood unlocked much of the time, even when facing a busy street.

Someone else in a relatively quiet quarter of the Clerkenwell police district also had a bad end to the year, though his case stands out from many similar ones only on account of his age and apparent respectability. This was Thomas Puny, a 52 year-old piano tuner, who was sighted by a passing policeman at 11.30 pm up against a wall in Barnsbury Park (a road) in close company with a 48-year-old woman described as a charwoman. Clearly, however, the magistrate knew her to be a frequent attender, as for 'indecency by having sexual intercourse contrary to LCC Bylaw' she was fined 40/-, alternative 1 month, whereas her customer only got 21/- or 14 days. The minute book reveals that, when accosted in a state of disarray, he ran off, pursued by the constable. "I caught him in Barnsbury Square, I told him the charge. He said 'Oh dear, this will kill me, I will give you £5 to square it.' I said no, I shall take you. He said 'You won't' and he clutched the iron railing. I took him to the station." Puny's evidence, that he had simply paused a moment when the woman accosted him, was not believed. At least he may have taken comfort from the fact that he was not charged with trying to bribe a police officer.

Poor Mr Puny might have found a more discreet place than the street. Although Barnsbury (an area of Islington west of the Liverpool Road, today much sought after by wealthy house buyers) was quieter and leafier in 1905 than Clerkenwell to the south, it was not wholly genteel. Earlier that year a lodging-house keeper at 47 Liverpool Road was prosecuted on the grounds that she was actually keeping a brothel. Police kept the place under continuous observation 'from 19th June to 25th', and testified that during that time 44 couples were seen to enter, of whom 34 'left after a short stay' and that no one had any luggage. One can only envy the police force of the time for having so much manpower that they could mount a round-the-clock watch for 6 days on such a routine matter.

The registers show a striking number of the homeless sleeping on the streets, mainly male and many of them not yet adult. This phenomenon would largely disappear after World War I, and become unthinkable after World War II for a generation – until, by the late 1980s, cheap or sheltered accommodation hardly existed any more. The police stopped arresting for vagrancy, having nowhere to send the vagrants, and the old problem of sleepers on pavements and in doorways came back. One case picked almost at random, from July

1905, may stand for many others: it could equally well be a case from the present day though not one that would now lead to the magistrates' court. Egbert Wallistow, 15 and described as 'a labourer with no visible means of support' was found by a constable asleep on a doorstep at Euston Buildings. 'Said he'd been turned out of home a fortnight ago. That he had been knocked about. He said he earned 7/6 for a week. . .' He was sent to a juvenile Remand Home (newly founded establishments for those between 14 and 16), but only for 7 days. Unlike the Court at Hampstead, where there were relatively few homeless, the Clerkenwell Court gives the impression of being at a loss to deal with the problem and the numbers involved.

Although magistrates' courts were still handling the traditional cases of wife desertion and bastardy arrears that would later be removed to the civil courts, there was little they could do but fine the errant man – not a particular useful procedure, or one likely to lead to greater marital harmony. The much rarer cases involving errant mothers were taken more seriously. There is no doubt that cruelty, neglect and *de facto* infanticide had been very common in poor homes throughout the 19th century, but one senses in the harrowing details of the case of Mary Ann Howard a growing social concern, and the first signs of a welfare infrastructure in the form of free advice and medicine.

In February 1906, Mary Ann, then aged 37, was accused of wilfully neglecting two of her children. She was arrested on a warrant and remanded in custody till the end of the week, when the case appears in the minute book under the heading 'Cruelty to Children'. It is not clear on whose information the arrest took place, but her husband, a corn chandler, was a principal witness against her: 'We have five children at home [including] Charles 1?, Sarah 4 months. . .I earn 23/- a week. I give my wife 17/-, one boy gives her 7/6.' (With over 30/- a week going into that household, the family was well above the lower levels of working-class poverty; Mary Ann should not have had a struggle to put food on the table.) 'In December the baby was ill, I asked her to take it to hospital she said Let it die. On 22 December [a Friday] she took it to University College Hospital. She brought back four packets each containing four powders. Baby was to have powder three times a day. She was to take baby again the following Friday. She said Let Baby die. She never gave baby the powders. On 19 January she got more packets.

The child kept poorly at home – been ill since 5 or 6 weeks of age. She let baby remain in bed. . . [Presumably the marital bed. A sentence is illegible here]. She was given clothes for the child, she pawned them. I offered to pay in clothing club for children. She refused to help and said, Let them go without clothing. Both children are now in the Infirmary.' He further revealed that he and Mary Ann had had between them 15 children but that 10 had died as babies. One of them, aged between 2 and 4 months, he did not remember the exact age, had weighed only 9 lb: 'They wasted away in starvation.'

The landlady testified: 'They [the Howards] have two rooms. I noticed the baby seemed sick, I said it ought to be taken to hospital. She said, I will see how it goes, it got worse. . . She said, Oh I am not going to take it to hospital. Baby cried very much. I spoke to her, she told me to mind my own business. . . Both the husband and the wife are sober.' [This last remark presumably in response to a question from the Bench, since the most obvious explanation was that the housekeeping money was going on drink.]

The husband stated in answer to further questions: 'My wife is in her right mind. Baby is insured at 1 shilling a week. [Insurance in a Burial Club is what is meant.] 'Seven out of ten of our children were insured. My wife paid the insurance. The funerals cost more, except in one case.'

The hospital doctor gave evidence. It may have been he who alerted the police: 'Baby is 4 months old, thin and emaciated, no fat about the body, private parts excoriated due to neglect, napkins wet. Had appearance of being very much neglected, starved. . . The elder child showed signs of rickets due to improper diet. . . Child dirty but not verminous.' A home visit was made and there were signs that the children were being fed scantily on bread and butter and tinned milk. The findings were corroborated by a second doctor, who agreed that 'the condition of the children was likely to cause them unnecessary suffering'. The defendant's husband had repeated in her presence his allegations about her failure to give the powders.

Mary Ann was convicted and condemned to 12 months' hard labour. It is unimaginable that, when she emerged from prison, domestic life would be taken up as before; her end is not likely to have been a happy one. One may justifiably see her, as the court did, as an 'unnatural mother', callous and hopelessly incompetent, someone the husband and surviving children would be better off without. Or one may equally see her as a pathetic victim of constant childbearing, tried beyond her mental and physical strength, severely clinically depressed. The record does not indicate what further arrangements were made for the two young children in the case. If the concerned neighbour or a female relative could not care for them when they emerged from the Infirmary, they would have been sent off initially to the children's Reception Home (a purpose-built modern alternative to the workhouse that had opened 2 years before in Kentish Town) and thence to the LCC children's home in Hertfordshire, to a country foster home, or to Dr Barnardo's famous establishment at Barkingside. Born into circumstances of still Dickensian squalor and privation, they may have grown up into a world where, before they were old, the Welfare State arrived to take responsibility for all their basic needs and those of their children and grandchildren.

Prosecutions in every era relate as much to the moral preoccupations of that era as to the trouble actually caused by the offences. Intimate practices on the Heath or in dark side streets were not invented by late Victorians; they were simply prosecuted then with a new vigour. Earlier generations had preferred to ignore them, as we do again today. In more specific areas of social control, every few years seems to produce a new focus of attention for the forces of law and order, which then disappears again from the books when something else seems more important. The spate of prosecutions for failing to muzzle dogs, which half filled the registers briefly at the end of the 19th century, may have been due to a rabies scare; at any rate, they had virtually disappeared a few years later. In a rather different way, the need to induce parents to have their children vaccinated, a preoccupation for many years before World War I, seemed to fade away after it even though the requirement was still on the statute book. Between the wars, out-of-hours drinking and illicit drinking clubs occupied much court time, with no one apparently speculating that the liquor laws might be unnecessarily strict. Much nearer our own time, fashions in prosecution for various motoring offences have come and gone.

Particularly odd to the modern browser through Edwardian registers seems the obsession with suppressing gambling – centuries' old behaviour which, it might be thought, caused no breach of public order and was of no possible consequence to anyone except the parties involved. The Clerkenwell registers of the 1900s are full of male groups, often adolescents, playing pitch and toss in quiet alleyways or 'cards for money'; other, similar charges appear to relate to street betting. But the middle and upper classes too played cards for money, legally, in the privacy of their own comfortable homes, and they bet on horses. A civilised disquiet had begun to make itself felt. Hugh R P Gamon, the young man financed by the Toynbee Trust, who published his findings in 1907 as *The London Police Court Today and Tomorrow*, wrote:

> Magistrates will be found to say in Court that they do not consider betting immoral. . .The very law seems curiously undecided and devoid of principle. . . as long as betting is openly tolerated anywhere it is not clear that it is fair to single out the street corner bookie. . . The street betting fraternity are committing a comparatively venial offence, and are a harmless set of men from the police point of view.

This was the Achilles heel of the police, since the current law led to protection rackets, with bookies appearing in court to pay £5 only every so often and otherwise being left in peace.

Gamon's book presents a clear picture of how the metropolitan police courts of the time were functioning. Much of his research was done at the Tower Bridge court in Southwark, but since this was another courthouse rebuilt by Dixon Butler at much the same time as Clerkenwell, and served a similar population, his general remarks are equally applicable to that court. His references to 'a dismal odour of unkempt and dirty humanity', and to the respectable man's indignation if ever he was forced to attend 'so disgraceful a place', echo the note of the 1840s, but other passages are more redolent of a late-Victorian high-mindedness. After remarking that 'As far as the textbooks are concerned the magistrate might be an automatic weighing machine', he goes on to explain that in practice the magistrate's functions 'are not wholly judicial. He is the authoritative teacher of the unwritten laws of morality. It is a wholesome thing that one sitting in a court, where most of those who come into contact with him have lower standards and ideals than himself, should deliver strong opinions where they are apposite and warranted. . .The elderly gentleman in the black frock coat, with firm lips and an expression of mild-eyed resignation. . .is the head and heart of the police court.'

The principal frock-coated gentleman in Clerkenwell Court was one E C Tennyson d'Eyncourt. His father – who must have been quite elderly when the son was born – was a stipendiary magistrate at the same court; he appears in the lists for 1842. E C, an Old Etonian barrister with a house in Lowndes Square and a country house in Lincolnshire, sat in Clerkenwell from 1897 for nearly 20 years, before moving to Marylebone and finally to Great Marlborough Street – the court that was memorably satirised as 'Mulberry Street' in Pinero's *The Magistrate*. The fact that, the year after his departure from Clerkenwell, the gaoler's returns record, for the first time, that no children were sentenced to be birched, presumably reflects a difference in views between him and his successor. During the 1920s, indeed, the enlightened began muttering that beating children did not seem to be any sort of deterrent.

E C Tennyson d'Eyncourt, Clerkenwell stipendiary magistrate 1897–1916

Gamon depicts a court very much dependent on police rather than civilian staff for its organisation and running; this would remain true for decades. Although so many cases were still brought by means of a private summons, the police were always on hand to deliver the summons and to advise. Later in the century most magistrates' court cases were presented by policeman, either by the arresting officer himself or by a sergeant designated for the job, and this lasted until the creation of the Crown Prosecution Service in 1984. 'The warrant officers keep order in the court-room and the hall, and assist the clerks with part of the clerical work; and they take it in turns, two and two at a time, to go out and issue summonses and execute warrants. . . And, if they cannot find the person they want during the day, they may be obliged to visit his house late at night and look round carefully lest he should be hiding under bedclothes or elsewhere.'

Warrant officers were also responsible for finding out from those who entered the front hall of the court, the main public space, what sort of application they wanted to make. Whereas today few people enter a courthouse without a previous exchange of paper between them or their solicitor and the Court, at that time the magistrate was often the first port of call for the distressed and aggrieved:

> Often applicants don't really know what they want and the magistrate has to advise.. promise to send a police constable to talk to the offender, or direct the parties to the civil court, or tell the applicant to go home and make it up. . .

Then, as still today in the older court buildings, the hall tended to become crowded with people whom it was not necessarily desirable to have rubbing up against each other. The busiest times were, as now, just before the 10 am and 2 pm sessions, and here Gamon's description has hardly dated:

> It is a motley assortment of applicants, prosecutors, witnesses, complainants, defendants, friends and loafers; bullies and their backers, sufferers and their sympathisers, husbands and wives, with their relations and neighbours and babies in arms... There are coarse faces with a truculent and defiant air; and frail, pale faces with an anxious and scared look, as if they feared the morrow.

He also remarked that while there were always a few people around being difficult, most appeared cowed by their situation. Between 50 and 75% of the defendants had no previous convictions and never reappeared. Some of the others were back all the time.

Magistrates and their police sheepdogs did, however, have another resource available to them by 1907, and that was the embryo probation officer. Known as 'court missionaries', these individuals had resulted in the later 19th century from an initiative by various churches. Under a Church of England outreach programme to offenders, the missionaries' original aim was to find convicted men and women at a low point in their lives and persuade them that by signing a temperance pledge they would transform their prospects for the better. The Church was right in thinking that alcohol lay at the root of much bad behaviour, but no one will be

surprised to hear that few pledges got signed in court halls and
fewer still were kept. However, the missionaries recognised the more
general need for someone about the court to sort out bureaucratic
confusions, find out more about a defendant's situation, explain and
admonish, lend a sympathetic ear and act as go-between. By 1907
there were more than 100 missionaries, working regularly though
not usually full-time, in about 200 courts in London and other big
cities. Gamon, who was thoroughly in favour of the missionary and
thought he ought to be called a Police Court Friend, wrote

> On his first entrance in the police court he was regarded with
> suspicion and distrust, as an intruder in police domains. He has
> now made himself a home in the court, and overcome much of
> the dislike; he may even have warm, sympathetic friends among
> the police. . . but he suffers from his anomalous position in the
> court. His uncertain rank, lacking its proper dignity, renders him
> liable to be disregarded.'

His rank was particularly uncertain in that he had, in theory, to
be paid by those who used his services, but in practice much of his
work of overseeing offenders was done for nothing. However, the
idea of rehabilitative probation as part of a sentence, first started in
Boston, Massachusetts, as a way of ensuring that a binding over was
kept, had been taken up in the UK by the Quakers of the Howard
Association (the forerunner of the Howard League for Penal
Reform). In the year that Gamon was writing, an Act made it
possible for magistrates to order payment from public funds to court
missionaries, soon to be known as probation officers, who provided
a service for first offenders. Gamon noted approvingly that both
Australia and the USA had already developed the idea of probation
as an *alternative* to other penalties. This was not yet the case in
England, but its desirability became obvious among progressive
thinkers in the years ahead. They could hardly have foreseen the
time when Treasury-driven pressures would deform the whole
meaning of the word 'probation', and the missionaries' original
benign intervention would be unrealistically described as 'a strict
sentence in its own right'.

Fines were now by far the commonest penalty, but about 20%
of those fined in London courts in 1907 went to prison for failure
to pay. Gamon remarked: 'Magistrates can only vary the fine within

comparatively narrow limits; and the rich man is not seriously inconvenienced by this discrimination, though the poor man, where it is a question of a shilling or two this way or that, may be saved from prison thereby.' He was touching on a problem of notional 'fairness' which has, in one way or another, exercised courts ever since – and, in recent years, led to a notoriously ill-advised and short-lived Home Office attempt to dictate fines entirely by income, without relation to the circumstances of the offence. Gamon was clearly in touch with the feeling of his times, for the Criminal Justice Administration Act of 1914 laid down that a defendant's means were to be taken into consideration when deciding the fine. However, it was still said more than a quarter of a century later that 'some magistrates feel they should not do this'.

★   ★   ★

For the 20th century, with full sets of registers and minute books available for both Hampstead and Clerkenwell, the vast amount of potential material available for research and comment induces vertigo. All this material is of the same obscure and fugitive kind, relating to the lost lives of innumerable individuals, a vast archive of human folly from the most diverting to the most desolating, which only cumulatively and in relation to other events acquires historical significance. If, then, I pick one week to stand for a whole decade of court activity, this is not because I have been able to select that week as particularly revelatory but because I have plucked it out like a handful of straw from a stack. This is not quite a random process, since certain dates carry a meaning imparted to them by other events in places far from the magistrates' Bench; but the registers themselves confirm that the law is above and beyond current events, whose reverberations reach the courtroom only like muffled thunder.

In the week beginning Monday 10 July 1916, the battle of the Somme was still in process, one of the most murderously pointless engagements of the huge slaughter that was World War I. In Clerkenwell Court E C Tennyson d'Eyncourt was still sitting, though this was to be his last year there. He had 30 charges before him that morning, of which 12 involved men who had either deserted from the armed forces while on leave or failed to present themselves at the appropriate office when their call-up had come – conscription had been introduced that year. All these men were handed over to an army escort squad which was apparently present in court. With the hindsight of history, one cannot help feeling that whatever their ultimate fate, the men's instinct in deserting had been a sound one. In addition, another man, a munitions worker, was charged with falsely representing himself to be a police constable and with attempting to obtain money by threats – presumably from other men hoping to avoid the escort. (He was discharged for lack of evidence.) Also two soldiers and an actress were respectively charged with larceny and receiving, involving 'army papers', draft books, army money orders and so forth. (They were all remanded on bail for trial by jury at a higher court.)

Otherwise, life in Clerkenwell was proceeding much as usual, except that it was rather calmer than it had been before the war because so many men were absent. Still, nine people had managed to get drunk and disorderly over the weekend, including one woman of 24 who pleaded guilty to being drunk in charge of a child under 7. (She was fined 10/6, which she apparently paid.)

Annie Hunn (aged 39) assaulted and beat Annie Crump. It was noted in the minutes that she was 'very sorry'. Bound over to keep the peace in the sum of £5 for 12 months.

A man of no fixed abode went to prison for 6 days for trying to get to Coventry by rail with only a platform ticket. He could have paid a 10/- fine instead, but presumably did not have it.

A brass finisher of 17 (too young for the army) was charged with begging near Euston station on the previous Saturday evening. He had been offering to carry luggage and when refused had asked for pennies. He had apparently been bailed till the Monday when he had dutifully appeared. Sentence, 1 day's custody – which would in practice be served simply by his staying within the courthouse till the end of the afternoon, a merciful provision much used in the 20th century at Clerkenwell as a means of dealing with the large floating population that the big stations attract.

A couple of domestic dramas centred on accusations of adultery, replete with such details as 'seized his wife by the hair and threw her down in the passage.' A 22-year-old railway porter was remanded on bail till the end of the week for stealing a pair of what sound like rather expensive boots. (When he reappeared on Friday he was fined 10/-, which he paid, but was apparently drunk and obstreperous. He too was handed over to the military.)

The following 14 days witnessed several more colourful marital disagreements: possibly, the conditions of war exacerbated tensions, particularly when a man had been absent and then returned. One of the husbands claimed 'I did not assault her. She keeps nagging and tantalising me.' There were two separate observations and raids of local brothels. An Australian soldier found in bed with a woman in one of them proved an unusually co-operative witness: 'The woman is not my wife. I came here with her for an immoral purpose. . . I picked her up in the street and gave her 21/- to pay for the room.'

A 20 year old cook concealed the birth of her child (committed for trial by jury). Two separate men committed bigamy, one of them 61 years old (trial by jury). Two men were convicted of cruelty to horses by working them when they were lame and worn out. Several servants were caught stealing butter and bacon, food now in short supply because of the war. A row in a pub centred on someone being called 'a f..... German'.

The railway stations often figure as convenient venues for theft, drunkenness, indecent behaviour between two males in a coach waiting in a siding, and (on 14 July) an attempt by a soldier, once again a deserter, to cut his own throat with a knife. He pleaded guilty and seems to have been bailed in the sum of £5 to reappear another day, but it is not clear that he did.

In early September two soldiers, a woman shorthand-typist and another woman were charged with forging army passes. This contested case occupies many pages in the minute book and seems to have been the result of an elaborate sting set up by the police. Everyone concerned went to prison. The following day one man was charged with 'falsely representing himself to be a person to whom an army classification certificate had been issued', and another with 'falsely representing himself to the recruiting authorities to be another person'. The war in one way or another was taking its toll.

8 Between the Wars

No one will be surprised to hear that wartime life in Hampstead was more peaceful than in sooty Clerkenwell, but the war was present all the same. In the register that covers the last year of that war (a register with the heading 'Petty Sessional Division of ...' firmly crossed out, and 'Hampstead Petty Sessional Court' substituted for it) numerous soldiers are recorded as up before the Bench. The Hampstead police seem to have preferred the charge 'AWOL' – absent without leave – to the stark 'Desertion', but the result was the same. The police took their duties regarding the war effort seriously, no doubt all too thankful that they were not in a position to be sent to France themselves, though some had volunteered, their places being filled by part-time special constables. One evening that same year, a strapping teenager (who was later to become my father-in-law) walking along the Spaniards Road was accosted by a constable, asked why he was not in the army, and escorted home to have his story verified. His father, a respected Hampstead tradesman, succeeded in convincing the policeman that his son was only 15.

The Court's other main preoccupation was with food regulations, which had been introduced late in the war in an attempt to prevent shortages from driving up prices. Defendants were charged with disobeying the Sugar (Domestic Preserving) Order, disobeying the Bread Order, the Meat (Maximum Prices) Order, and the Beans, Peas and Pulses (Retail Price) Order. Various failures among householders to 'reduce and shade' lights also attracted penalties, usually as high as 20/-: the blackout which was to be such a feature of World War II was not required, but only dim lights were tolerated, for fear of Zeppelins. Very few defendants were sent to prison, but a few were charged for failing to conform with the Aliens Act, for instance 'being a Belgian refugee', or Chinese and failing to notify a change of address.

Among so many dreary charges that were offences only because of the war, it comes as quite a relief to find that more traditional offences were still being pursued with enthusiasm, including indecency on the Heath. When one couple was arrested in September 1917, the man said indignantly 'The special constables are a dammed lot of skunks. I wasn't doing any harm.'

The special sessions of cases concerning juveniles, which

Hampstead court had begun 20 years before, were now marked in
the minutes as 'Juvenile Court'. This did not imply a separate court
with its own procedures, but a hearing for juveniles only held on
a different day from the adult court, which was in session two or
three times a week by this time. Since 1908, no-one under 14 could
be sent to prison, but there were many other institutions for older
teenagers, including the new Borstals. Hampstead Justices seem
to have taken the concept of probation to heart; indeed one entry
in the minutes for 1918 reads 'Miss Sarah Brind of Lawn Road and
James Nunn of Buxton reappointed as Probation Officers', so the
system was in place there long before the employment of probation
officers became, theoretically, compulsory some years after the war.
The Hampstead Bench were using probation by this time as a
complete disposal: for instance, in April 1918, for stealing a purse
with 10/6 in it, a 15-year-old boy was given 6 months' probation,
and another got the same treatment for 'embezzling various sums of
money' – a far cry from the beatings that would have been ordered
in the 1880s or '90s. However, these were presumably first offenders,
for another boy at the very same session was to be given six strokes
of the birch rod as 'a suspected person, attempting to steal' and was
to be sent to an Industrial School for 3 years – presumably a known
bad boy the town wished to be rid of. Another, convicted for stealing
from his employer (Forsters, the High Street grocer) was sent to a
reformatory. Both of these disposals may have been intended as
essentially rehabilitative. The magistrate, a Dr Macdonald Brown,
noted in the minute for the shop thief 'Lad's eyesight not good'.

Who were the Hampstead Justices during the war? There
seem to have been 7 or 8 active ones, including the doctor, a Henry
Bleasby, a W H Pitman and an Andrew T Taylor. This last was
a distinguished architect and academic who eventually received
a knighthood. He retired to Hampstead, which he represented on
the LCC for many years; he was mayor of the town at one time,
and on innumerable committees redolent of the great, the good
and the liberal. He lived at Drummond Lodge in Lyndhurst Road,
conveniently near the magistrates' court. He had a neat, pointed
beard like King George V and favoured tweed suits and light-
coloured waistcoats, at a date when his presumably more
conventional contemporary, Dr Macdonald Brown, was still in
the black jacket, striped trousers and wing collar of the prosperous
practitioner. I know these details about the learned magistrates'

dress because I have a photograph of the Hampstead magistrates (*below*) taken on a summer's day in Andrew Taylor's garden.

The picture is dated 1924, so a few years had passed since the end of the war. Various changes in the magistracy were now underway. Women magistrates had first been appointed in 1919; by 1924 their numbers had grown to about 1000 (total number of JPs in England and Wales, about 25,000), and continued to grow thereafter. Three out of the Hampstead Bench of (apparently) 10, were now women, a proportion far above the national average. They were Lady Byles, who was the widow of a prominent Liberal MP (long silk coat-frock, hat, feather boa, walking stick), Mrs M A Monro (ample black silk, old-fashioned ostrich feather hat) and Mrs M W Nevinson (summer coat, a hat of course, but hints of bohemianism in a scarf tied gypsy-style round her neck and in her light sandal-style button shoes).

Margaret Wynne Nevinson, who was, among other things, the mother of C W R Nevinson the war artist, was a force to be

The Hampstead magistrates photographed in 1924 in the garden of the chairman, Andrew Taylor. *Left to right, back row*: W J Ruegg, Chas T Green, W Ewart Price. *Front row*: Lady Byles, Mrs M W Nevinson, Dr J MacDonald Brown, Frank G Howard (Mayor), L J Sloan, Mrs M Monro, R H Hammersley-Heenan, (Sir) Andrew Taylor

reckoned with. Described in *Who's Who* as 'public speaker and writer' she has left us an autobiography called *Life's Fitful Fever*, which provides a lively insight into the life of the progressive New Woman in the late 19th and early 20th century. Born about 1860, the daughter of a prominent clergyman of the Oxford Movement, and of a mother who tolerated education for her daughter but said that no one would marry a girl who knew Greek, Margaret Wynne longed to go to Girton, then newly founded. But her father was by then dead and with two brothers at Oxford there was no further money for the daughter. She got a teaching job at South Hampstead High School for Girls, and studied for a London University law degree in the evenings – 'There were no clubs or hostels for girls then, and I sometimes found my lodgings rather lonely.' She was attracted culturally to the 'greenery-yallery Grosvenor gallery' movement that followed pre-Raphaelitism; she was also drawn into the moderate branch of the women's suffrage movement, which became a lifetime's cause for her.

In her mid-20s, she married H W Nevinson, who had connections with the old Hampstead family the Woodds. He was a journalist and foreign correspondent, and he too left an autobiography. The young couple lived for two years in a tenement block in Whitechapel, exercising practical charity under the auspices of Toynbee Hall and Canon Barnett. After their second child was born the Nevinsons compromised with their ideals, fearing that their infants would 'pick up slum habits'. They moved to 'a tumbledown old shack in John Street' (now Keats Grove), and there followed a long life for Margaret Wynne devoted to good causes, political campaigns, street corner speaking, enthusiastic bicycling and, increasingly, crusading journalism of her own. By the time she was appointed to the Bench in 1920, aged about 60, she had served on LCC education committees and had been for many years a Poor Law Guardian. Because of the unique nature of the Hampstead Bench, she was the first woman ever to sit in a court of criminal jurisdiction within the London area. She had not expected to be appointed when her name was put forward, as 'there were several anti-suffrage ladies on the Lord Chancellor's advisory committee'. When she heard she was, she hastened to Hampstead Court to enquire when she might be needed?

'I found only a young policeman on duty, who confidently assured me that 'lady magistrates' never sat on the Hampstead

Bench. I told him that times had changed, that in future they would do so. "Oh dear," said the man, "I don't know what we shall do. This is one of the worst courts in the country, Hampstead Heath is a very wicked place and dreadful things go on there. I don't think I can say what it is my duty to say in front of any lady"; and his honest face flushed crimson at the thought.'

When she began to sit, to her relief she was received courteously by the gentlemen of the Bench, to most of whom she must have been known already through her Poor Law work. 'Our then Chairman, Dr Macdonald Brown, confessed later, at a public dinner, he had been very apprehensive as to what might happen with a woman Justice there; but added to my great satisfaction that he had been agreeably surprised to find that a woman's knowledge and experience were a real asset on the Bench.'

A similar tribute was paid by the Lord Chancellor in 1924 when he was addressing the Magistrates' Association (formed 3 years earlier, mainly on the initiative of the Quaker and first-ever woman JP Margery Fry): 'I am sure there is no occupant of a Bench here today who does not feel that in certain cases he is glad to have a woman magistrate sitting with him and helping with that knowledge which man does not aspire to, and probably can never completely attain.' Today's women JPs would hardly be delighted with such partial and patronising accolades, but these do indicate the huge shifts of opinion that had taken place within Margaret Wynne's active lifetime. As she wrote herself, apropos of the protection that married women might or might not receive under the criminal law (a subject close to her heart), 'Nothing is more encouraging than to read old diaries and notes of 20 years ago and realise the enormous progress.'

Neither she nor her male colleagues could possibly have envisaged that in the London area, by the late 20th century, woman Justices would outnumber men and sometimes sit with no male colleague present – a situation good neither for justice nor for the appearance of justice, since the great majority of defendants are, as ever, male.

Between the wars and for long after, many of the cases that would now be heard in civil courts or in special Domestic Court sessions were still part of the magistrates' ordinary fare: separation and maintenance orders, paternity orders, arbitration in matrimonial offences. The traditional penalty for deserting wife and children had been a month in gaol, which hardly solved anyone's problem. By Margaret Wynne Nevinson's day, however, these sorts of cases were at last being dealt with as humanitarian issues, rather than being driven by the simple desire that the abandoned family should not become a charge upon the rates. She remarked: 'Very often the Court Sergeants are sent to advise, warn and admonish in the many domestic brawls, generally with good results. These men, often, have such gifts of tact and peacemaking, that one feels they would have been ideal Bishops and are a real loss to the Church.'

This was, you may say, the Bench and its servants still behaving in the time-honoured way as community peacekeepers. In other ways, however, the magistracy continued to move further from its traditional role into the judicial one. This transition, begun in the 1850s, was more or less complete when the Criminal Justice Act of 1925 shifted into the magistrates' courts another swathe of offences that had previously been dealt with only by a judge and jury. Throughout the 20th century and to the present day, the tendency of government has been to move in this direction, in an attempt first to take pressure off the Quarter Sessions and later the Crown Courts. The relentless rise in reported crime since the ending of the first world war has meant, however, that the intended effect has never been achieved.

In 1924 the amount of crime known to the police was greater than at any time since the early 1860s. As correspondents to the Magistrates' Association journal regularly pointed out, this sustained rise was partly due to 'the increased willingness of victims, or of those interested in them, to report certain classes of offence'. Offences associated with cars, of which there were more on the roads each year, also went to swell the figures. By 1930 there had been what was described as a 'huge rise' in housebreaking, as burglars began to travel for the first time into lonely country areas. Thefts from cars began to be a preoccupation too, motor vehicles being left unattended in a way horse-drawn ones never had been.

Not all types of case had shown an increase in the post-war years. At a Women Magistrates' Conference held in April 1925, discussion turned to prostitution, the unfairness of the way the law leant on the women as opposed to their customers (still, today, an issue), and the way the police over-used the charge of 'riotous and indecent behaviour' to arrest prostitutes. All the same, it was agreed that only about 5000 a year were then being arrested in the

metropolitan area, whereas for the year 1908 the figure had been
11,000 – 'and I do not think anybody would say the conditions in
our streets are worse.' Three reasons are offered for this happy state
of affairs: that street lighting was better, that 'public opinion
demands a better standard of conduct in the streets than it did 20
years ago', and 'the presence of respectable women in our streets
at all hours of the day and night.' One might also add, with the
hindsight of history, that life for the poorest was not as hard as
it had once been, and fewer women were driven to sell themselves
through sheer destitution. Since the war, there were more jobs
available to them, and the old, grudging system of Poor Relief was
gradually changing to that of insurance-based benefits. (Widows'
pensions were introduced in 1925.) 'Settlements' such as Toynbee
Hall had spread their message; in areas like Clerkenwell, day
nurseries, free Infant Welfare Clinics and Health Centres (including
a famous early one in Finsbury) had begun to have their effect.

We are far, here, from the Darkest London of mid-Victorian
writers; quite far, too, from the female drunkenness and street
brawls of Edwardian Clerkenwell. But the popular image of the area
was still far from encouraging. Margaret Wynne Nevinson mentions
being sworn in as a magistrate in 'one of the dirtiest courts of dirty
old Clerkenwell', and the King's Cross Road gets a mention in
Arnold Bennett's *Riceyman Steps* (1923) as 'a hell of noise and dust
and dirt, with the County of London tramcars, and motor-lorries
and heavy horse-drawn vans sweeping north and south in a vast
clangour of iron thudding and grating on iron and granite'. Just
down the road from the courthouse, a huge red-brick Rowton
House had been built earlier in the century, and this is referred
to as 'divided into hundreds and hundreds of clean cubicles for the
accommodation of the defeated and the futile.' (The same site is
currently occupied by a gaunt hotel from the Holiday Inn chain,
patronised mainly by foreign tourists, while the defeated and the
futile have returned to the streets from which the efforts of several
generations had previously rescued them.)

Bennett's view of the area was typical of his time, when almost
all such old London districts were viewed by the educated classes as
hideous, depressing and ripe for some as yet unspecified abolition.
The distant suburb was rapidly becoming the home area of choice
for every class but the unskilled workers. The one-time middle-class
houses on the Lloyd Baker estate on the Islington side were now in

multi-occupation, and it is true that the LCC boroughs of Holborn and Finsbury and the southern part of St Pancras, all of which fell within the jurisdiction of Clerkenwell court, had some of the highest crime rates in London. But many of these supposed crimes, particularly among juveniles, were still of a footling boys-will-be-boys kind, such as scrawling 'indecent words' on walls or playing football in the street. The register and minute books for the late 1920s do not present a picture of the courts and alleys of Clerkenwell as sunk in their old ways, but of a district evolving as all such urban districts do.

Although drunkenness and assault and domestic disharmony still appear in the register, cases were noticeably fewer than before. Instead, as an index of an increasing sense of respectability among the working classes, bigamy had now become quite a frequent crime. But the commercial nature of central Clerkenwell was now attracting more substantial crimes of dishonesty – breaking and entering shops, theft of wallets and suitcases, receiving of stolen jewellery, and business fraud. For example, in January 1928 a clerk was convicted of embezzling twice over from his employer the sum of £20.6.6, and sentenced by stipendiary Samuel Pope to 3 months on each charge, 6 months in all, then as now the maximum magistrates' court sentence. In the same month Alex Cohen, a 'gown manufacturer' of Goswell Road aged only 17, was accused of 'wilfully and maliciously setting fire to workshop with intent to injure and defraud'. He was remanded on bail with a surety, but as the magistrate's subsequent decision does not appear in that register the case must have been continued before a different magistrate, which frequently happened now that cases were examined with more care and deliberation. A second courtroom had now been built on the yard behind the older part of the building to enable two court-sittings to run simultaneously.

The extent to which parts of Clerkenwell were now given over to the garment trade (a burgeoning industry, in those inter-war years of more readymade clothes and cheaper materials) is clear from a number of thefts from warehouses, and one of a Morris Cowley car containing 92 ladies' dresses, 15 coats and 107 coathangers.

A number of charges at this time, both in Clerkenwell and in Hampstead, were for 'being drunk in charge of a motor car'. Since traditionally, *drunk* had always meant 'visibly and incapably drunk' (as in the police mantra 'His gait was unsteady, your worships, his

speech was slurred, his breath smelt of alcohol'), it took a while for
society and the courts to come to terms with the fact that you could
be more or less sober for ordinary purposes but in no condition to
drive. A Bill amending the wording of the charge was finally passed
in 1930. Throughout the 1920s, earlier war injuries or records were
often invoked to excuse this and other offences, which indicates the
extent to which the traumatic slaughter in the trenches remained in
everyone's consciousness. For instance, a taxi driver at Clerkenwell
in 1928 'stated that his condition. . .was due to war injuries, not
to two glasses of beer he had had.' In January 1930 a Clerkenwell
brick-checker accused of exposing himself 'with intent to insult
a female', was sent by the magistrate to see a doctor. The minutes
of the next magistrate before whom he appeared, a well-respected
Mr Clarke-Hall, record: 'Dr reports of low intelligence, but not
certifiable as insane or MD. On 26.4.13 three months [custody] for
similar but nothing since. . .Married, 4 children, 9 to 19 years, v.
good character at work, served 4 years in war. Further remand on
bail on condition will take medical advice.' Times were certainly
changing.

Some of the magistrates of this period, as well as their
customers, were ex-war veterans. By a happy chance, no fewer
than three men who were Clerks at Clerkenwell (Stanley French,
F T Giles and Derek Wainwright) at various periods between the
1930s and the 1970s have left books of reminiscences behind them,
complete with vivid portraits of the more colourful and now safely
dead magistrates for whom they clerked. It is a court Clerk's fate,
for most of his life, to allow magistrates to have their head without
comment, except for proffering strictly legal advice. No wonder if,
on final retirement, he is possessed by an overwhelming desire to say
what he has been forced to bite back for decades. Today, Clerks are
as highly qualified as the barristers who sit as stipendiaries, and
similarly well paid, but when F T Giles and Stanley French started
out almost haphazardly on the career paths that led them eventually
to the top of their profession, Giles after World War I and French
a decade later, each made his way in the courts service with little
initial legal training. Even Derek Wainwright, coming a generation
later, after World War II, had a somewhat chequered start, as if the
best and most enduring Clerks only arrive in that niche by accident.

French's *Crime Every Day* gives an interesting overview of the
London police courts of the 1930s, '40s and '50s, but his view of

Clerkenwell court, where he was never a permanent member of staff, is the conventional one of his times: 'It always seemed a depressing court in a decaying neighbourhood. . .When in 1952 I transferred the hearing of the Christie committal from West London to the second court at Clerkenwell I felt I was providing a suitable atmosphere for the first telling of that macabre story.' [Christie was the mass murderer and necrophiliac who hid the bodies of his victims in a kitchen cupboard in 10 Rillington Place, North Kensington.] Rather different was the perspective of Giles, who was Chief Clerk at Clerkenwell from 1933 to 1951 except for a brief period in the Juvenile court service during World War II. He obviously loved Clerkenwell ('a happy court'), while taking a sardonic view of its 'ponderous' size and architecture and the number of anxious people who had toiled up and down its hard-wearing granite front steps since 1905: 'Inside you will find an oak-panelled hall with a tessellated floor and here and there a choice selection of ratepayers' stained glass in pleasing shades of pale green and blue.' He also mentions the ornate plasterwork, complete with fruit shapes, that decorates the ceilings of both courts, a pleasant distraction for the straying eyes of generations of magistrates during boring motoring or rates lists.

F T Giles's acumen leads him to the heart of a problem which has haunted police courts from their beginning. Unrestrained by the presence of a jury or by colleagues from the bar, 'the single judge does make for singularity. Once upon the Bench…a man's characteristics are magnified fortyfold, like a slide thrown upon a screen from a magic lantern. If he is good, he is very, very good. If he is bad, he can be horrid.' We are back here with Dickens's magistrate Fang, in various latter-day incarnations. Giles is too diplomatic, and too debonair, to say exactly what he thinks of some decisions he has seen taken in court, but from the praise he bestows on the best magistrates you can see what he thinks of the worst ones.

He also makes the point that in his early years many metropolitan stipendiaries had gained their posts not through suitability but (like the lay magistrates of old) through an Old Boy network and family connections. Such a one, he intimates, was Arthur Gill who presided at Clerkenwell in the 1920s but whom he, Giles, encountered at other courts. Arthur Gill had seen 4 years' war service in the trenches, as had the robust F T Giles himself: one is inclined to wonder if the magistrate's experiences there had turned this apparently well-intentioned and sensitive man into a nervous wreck. When his own brother, a more flourishing lawyer, heard of Arthur Gill's appointment to the metropolitan courts, he exclaimed 'God help the Clerks!' Giles comments that Arthur Gill was:

> The only magistrate I ever knew who was unhappy in his work. All the others were no happier or unhappier in themselves than the rest of us, but they applied themselves to their appointed missions with zeal. . .[His] nervousness and indecision made him quite unsuitable for a tribunal where dispatch and incisiveness were essential. . .A tallish, slender man with delicate, feminine features and a pessimistic moustache. Always he held tight to a pair of pince-nez as others cling to a crucifix. He was always doing something with them – combing out his moustache, scratching his tall forehead and in moments of unusual stress even biting them.

Hardly less eccentric was 'Sam' Pope, whom Giles describes as a Victorian, Pickwickian figure, endlessly garrulous, who loved to argue with the Clerks – 'Sam was a bachelor approaching seventy when I came to Clerkenwell and I was assured that he was a virgin.' Nevertheless, he was given to deadpan, Rabelaisian jokes which the press – there were always boy reporters in court in those days – sometimes took seriously. He took to asking Giles to cough to stop him saying anything too unwise, but it was difficult to produce a cough in time to repress him.

One of Giles's most esteemed magistrates, who comes in for high praise also from Stanley French, was Bertrand Watson, later Chief Magistrate at Bow Street. At the opposite extreme from Pope, he was a man of few words but always fair and polite. Both Giles and French remark on his unusual habit of saying 'The court finds' or 'The court sentences you to. . .' when most solo magistrates would use 'I'. French remarks, 'Being tried by him must have seemed like being tried by a well-washed Buddha whose kindly instincts were visible beneath its divine detachment.'

Later magistrates Giles knew were Walter Hedley, who once witnessed bullets fired in his court by a white man summoned for an assault on three diminutive black men; and J H Broderick ('Old Brod'), who had a particularly courteous way of hearing the defendant out before delivering a disappointingly heavy sentence.

Then there was Herbert Metcalfe: 'Never have I seen a man who looked so like a pouter pigeon. . .his chest amplified by an overflowing silk cravat of the kind sported by Regency bucks.' But either discretion inhibited Giles as his account came nearer to the present or there were fewer picturesque characters about. In his earlier days as a junior clerk at Lambeth court, he had known one magistrate who used to sit when drunk and another who fell asleep with his feet on the Bench. He had even, as late as the 1950s, had to suffer the occasional presence in Clerkenwell of an elderly magistrate sent over from West London who was notoriously senile. The same figure of clerkly dread and embarrassment appears in Derek Wainwright's *A Clerk's Tale*. But Giles concluded on his retirement in the 1960s: 'The magistrate of today is a far better man than his predecessor of 1920, far better informed, far more conscientious, far more considerate.' Fang was at last routed. Or was he?

JP courts have their own built-in safeguard against abuse of power. In the 20th century Justices have normally sat in threes (this was established as a fixed principle after World War II), and therefore monitor and curb each others' more flagrant defects. Many of the 20th-century revisions of the concept of justice originated from lay magistrates rather than stipendiary ones, and many of the reforming ideas may be glimpsed in the pages of *The Magistrate*, the organ of the Magistrates' Association.

Today the Magistrates' Association is a large organisation without political orientation which all magistrates are encouraged to join, but in its early years it definitely represented the more liberal end of the spectrum. Though relatively weak in numbers, it pioneered certain ideas, such as probation, which were then taken up more widely and eventually became Home Office policy. It also invented and organised the whole idea of *training* voluntary magistrates, which now falls under the Lord Chancellor's department. To read through months and years of *The Magistrate* is to see the force of 'progressive', Hampstead-style thought in action. Yet individuals are never entirely the innovative spirits they seem to themselves and others but, rather, reflect something more deep-seated that one can only call the spirit of the times. A 1932 article in *The Magistrate*, entitled 'The Case for the Psychiatrist in Court', shows the lie of the land then: 'The attitude to crime has changed so greatly in recent years that it should not be difficult to satisfy the readers of this paper that there is an excellent case for enabling magistrates to call upon a psychiatrist. . .to examine and report on offenders.'

The day when it would become almost impossible to send anyone to prison for the first time without obtaining a full report on their mental health and circumstances still lay 60 years in the future, in 1991. Almost as far off lay a number of other developments, such as the extension of full legal aid to the magistrates' courts, the intervention of the Crown Prosecution Service between police and defendant, the presumption of the right to bail except in certain specified circumstances, the now general practice of allowing time to pay off fines without the threat of custody, and the virtual abandonment of certain classes of charges on the grounds that their relative triviality simply does not warrant the amount of paperwork they involve. If one looks back at the court registers for the 1930s, '40s and even '50s they look rather quaint, 'summary' in every sense of the word. And yet, by the standards of the generation earlier, and all the generations before that, they were thoroughly modern registers. They reflect a world we recognise as our own.

" 'Slash' Waters, a burly Liverpudlian member of the Euston Square
drinking fraternity, whipped off his left shoe and with a sweeping
movement lobbed it like a keen cricketer. . .the iron-tipped heavy
shoe crashed into the oak panelling of Clerkenwell Court I. The
missile was in a direct line with the Magistrate's head but the
trajectory was just an inch too high. As I saw on my last visit to
Clerkenwell in 1987, the dent in the oak panel behind the
Magistrate's chair was still visible. 'Slash' was one of the few of
the rotating stage army of local criminals to leave his mark on the
court."

So writes Derek Wainwright in *A Clerk's Tale*. No book about
the court would be complete without a reference to this episode
(which I think dates from the end of the 1960s), for the dent in the
panelling is indeed there to this day, in the shut and silent
courthouse. The magistrate in question was Mr Purcell, an august
personage whom many magistrates still sitting will remember.

Here arises a dilemma that cannot be solved within the limits
of this short book. The interest and meaning of any court's past
arises from the way in which the life of that court mirrors the
evolving society it serves; but once the historian nears the present
day, and considers the experiences of magistrates and court staff
who are still with us, the perspective shortens to the point at which
no clear view can be taken.

A generally held modern view would be that an accelerated
development and change took place after the second world war and
in the ensuing decades, with large amounts of legislation designed
to cope with the modern world. Yet it is too soon to analyse how
much of this legislation was of long-term significance and how much
of it essentially transient. The fact is that, for all the emphasis on
'progress' and change in 20th-century social thinking, far greater
real changes took place in the functioning of the magistracy in the
19th century than in the 100 years after.

The whole concept of progress is itself something of a trap.
Because everyone alive today in Britain has been brought up to
think that present-day society is fairer, more just and 'enlightened'
than that of our grandparents or great-grandparents, we are not well
placed to evaluate how genuine this progress has been or what may

have been sacrificed to it. This is not to say that changes in social and judicial practice over the last 50 years have necessarily been misguided: it is simply to state that we cannot yet tell, and that it is not realistic to recount the story of the magistrates' courts as a one-directional journey out of the Bad Old Days into the Good. Nor is it realistic to take the opposite view, fulminating against the procedural changes and harking back to some mythic past of a docile, respectful England when the courts and their clients functioned properly.

As we have seen, crime rates fell in the second half of the 19th century and the first two decades of the 20th, in spite of all the new crimes that had been placed on the statute book. The Victorian mission to turn Britain into a more peaceful, law-abiding and civilised society was, in some ways, very successful. The fall began to be reversed after World War I and the rise has continued, with peaks and troughs, ever since – but, as has been repeatedly pointed out, the population has not become more innately wicked: the opportunities and temptations to crime are now more extensive. At the same time, the preoccupation with social justice and equality, however well-intentioned, has had the cumulative effect of slowing court procedures down, thereby producing other kinds of injustice.

Especially in the last two decades of the 20th century, magistrates' courts have been battling with rising tides of paper, and often conflicting demands about the way they should deliver justice. Long delays have become endemic; cases that, a generation ago, were simple and speedy, have become so weighed down with safeguards and requirements that the essential nature of summary justice is in danger of being submerged. For an ordinary case of theft, say, to take 6 months to progress through the system, with half a dozen adjournments for legal, medical and psychiatric advice, exchange of papers, fixing of non-effective (i.e. token) dates and so forth, usually at public expense, before finally coming to court for trial, is agreed to be in absolutely no one's interest. But what can be done about this is not clear.

The crime rate rose during World War II and the years of austerity immediately after it, even though many men were away in the armed services; for that war, like the first, produced a mass of emergency laws concerned with such matters as blackout regulations, misuse of government petrol and black-marketeering. There were also prosecutions for looting from bombsites, which was strictly forbidden but which often, in practice, involved the rescue of

objects which would otherwise just spoil and be thrown away.
There was no coherence of view among Benches about whether
the penalty for this should be light or severe, and in general, as in
the earlier war, magistrates obliged to administer wartime
restrictions did not make themselves popular.

The situation was not helped by the fact that many of the
younger, abler magistrates or potential magistrates were themselves
away in the forces or heavily occupied in essential work, and the
Benches tended therefore to be in the hands of tired, over-stretched
old-timers. By 1945, Andrew Taylor, Dr Macdonald Brown,
Margaret Wynne Nevinson and their Hampstead colleagues of the
1920s were mostly dead and gone, but throughout the country more
than a quarter of all lay Justices were over 70. The extent to which
such Justices, who would have grown to full adulthood under the
reign of Victoria, were inadequate to the fast-changing world in
which they found themselves, may be judged by a row about dress
in court which erupted at the height of the war. In December 1943
the editor of the Magistrates' Association journal regretted that 'a
magistrate's recent remarks about a young woman witness appearing
before the Bench in trousers [at that time standard wear for many
war-workers] should have been treated in the press and elsewhere as
a matter rivalling in importance the progress of the Allied Armies in
Russia and Italy and even the release of Mosley.' In the next issue,
of January and February, the topic was still a live one: 'Magistrates
make themselves merely ridiculous if they utter protests which
simply show that they are a little slow to move with the times. We
may not like it, but we have got to accept the hatless, the trousered
or the bare-legged woman and the least said about it the better.'

Note that this was not an argument about what women
magistrates should wear, since they were all still behatted to a
woman. The woman the fuss was about was simply a witness, but
women were expected then to wear hats in court, even when they
were just in the public gallery. What would that traditionalist
magistrate have said if he could have looked forward another 40
years and seen, for instance, the Clerk's female secretary at
Hampstead coming into the court to give him some papers, wearing
what appeared to be a giant Babygrow suit? Or the young female
usher (another post-1950s innovation like the women Clerks) going
bra-less under a T-shirt on a hot summer's day? In fairness, both
these types of garb caused adverse comment at the time, and were

modified. ('Mrs Blenkinsop, I wonder if *you* could have a word with
our little usher? I feel it would come better from you, being a
woman.') The magistrate of the preceding generation would also,
I think, be dismayed to see that most of the court policemen have
now gone. Their often fatherly figures (paunches, half-moon glasses)
and their years of expertise in dealing with people have been
replaced by Crown Prosecution Service lawyers on the one hand
and ordinary security officers on the other. The atmosphere in court
is not the same, the place is less populated and bustling; the press
box is usually empty, for what local paper these days would bother
to send a reporter to listen to what might well be a string of bail
applications and adjournments? Only the language remains fixed,
the time-honoured phrases that remind one of older, harsher
realities –'gaoler's returns', 'man of previous good character',
'causing an affray', 'such as to cause a reasonable person to go
in fear', 'common prostitute', 'swear by Almighty God.'

Shortly after the war, during the late 1940s, there were several
well-publicised instances in which Benches of lay magistrates
outside London took quite unorthodox or actually illegal decisions,
apparently misled by their Clerks for various improper reasons. The
Clerks concerned were dealt with – but it became apparent that
too many magistrates, including chairmen of Benches, had little
notion of their real obligations and simply relied on their Clerks for
everything. Moves were set going to get rid of very elderly chairmen
and other magisterial dead wood, and for the first time in hundreds
of years there was a sustained attempt to eradicate the practice of
bestowing the title of 'Justice of the Peace' as an honour bringing
few duties in its wake.

There were also renewed attempts to broaden the basis of the
magistracy to include a wider social range. There was nothing very
new about this idea: already before 1914 a Commission had
recommended that 'working men with a first-hand knowledge of the
conditions of life among their own class should be appointed', and
between the wars nominations to the Bench from Trades Unions
brought in a few of these. But well after World War II, by which time
political nomination was in any case out of favour, not much had
changed. It still has not to this day, for the simple reason that the
very qualities of intelligence and competence that enable someone
to function well as a magistrate are those that make a person no
longer classifiable as working-class, even if he or she started out that

way. A much-valued member of Hampstead Bench in the 1970s and '80s regarded it as a matter of pride that he had begun work in Euston parcels office at the age of 14. But his modest beginnings had long been succeeded by a post of responsibility and influence within British Rail.

Once immigration had made a significant alteration to the population of London and other big cities, there were also attempts to get Justices from ethnic minorities. By the 1960s, Hampstead – in the vanguard as ever – had two black magistrates, Dr (later Lord) Pitt and Pauline Crabbe, prominent in social work circles. It has to be said, however, that both these popular JPs were noticeably middle-class and well educated. Within a few years, the Chief Clerk in Clerkenwell was of West Indian origin, but he was not famous for any noticeable understanding of the problems of his own people.

In the mid-1950s, the Hampstead Bench was still sitting regularly only on Mondays and Wednesdays, with extra days added as needed. It is a measure of the increasing workload that by 1960 it was sitting every weekday and on Saturday morning, though it is not apparent how often the work went over into the afternoon since no separate 2pm list was scheduled. Even when afternoon sittings became normal in the 1970s, Hampstead, unlike every other London court, allowed magistrates half-day sittings, and some of its busier members, among them local lawyers by that date, usually opted for these.

It is hard to tell from the registers the size of the Bench at any given time, since only the justice presiding in the chair signed the register, but there must have been many more magistrates to fill all these sittings than the dozen or so of earlier decades. Hampstead court maintained its long-standing reputation as a place with rather high-quality magistrates inclined to progressive views – 'rather a kind court', one retired magistrate remembers. 'When someone was up on a vagrancy charge we always gave them one day in custody so that they would get a free lunch.' But the same person also recalled that a fellow woman justice, the wife of a local headmaster, 'was very racially prejudiced. . .She was very fat, too, and made me cringe.' Perhaps it was lucky in this particular instance that women magistrates, still in a minority then, rarely took the chair in court – 'Before formal selection for chairmanship came in, it was just sort of assumed that a man would do it.'

But in the continual drive to 'raise standards' – more

specialised, separate Benches for Juvenile and Domestic/Family courts, more training for lay magistrates – the one major change of the post-war decades was brought about by the Criminal Justice Administration Act of 1965. This, together with the reorganisation of the numerous London County Council Boroughs into the larger and more widespread Greater London Council ones, led to the creation of the Inner London Magistrates' Courts Service. For the first time since the original public offices had been set up over 150 years before, the Middlesex Justices (now going under various different names according to the different parts of London they represented) were incorporated into courts which till then had been served entirely by stipendiaries. Considering that the trend for the previous 15 years had been against amateurism and political appointment, both of which were heavily represented among the under-employed London Justices, it was a remarkably radical move.

'It was chaos!' a Clerk cheerfully remembers. 'On the Hampstead Bench we suddenly got these extra people coming up from St Pancras Town Hall who'd never sat on anything but liquor-licensing cases and had done no training, and here they were let loose on crime. They didn't know whether they were coming or going. X [a one-time mayor of the borough] couldn't grasp the difference between committal proceedings and a trial and used to announce "We find the case proved" when the Bench had only been asked to say if there was a case to answer. We also had one who tried to fine people who had merely come to court to be bound over.'

The crisis was particularly acute on the Hampstead Bench because its lay magistrates sat on every kind of case. In the other London courts, where stipendiaries had till then always presided, the new magistrates were shuffled into the least important cases and were only gradually suffered to play a fuller role. But Hampstead's situation, as ever, was strange. On paper, it henceforth formed half of the West Central Division of the Inner London Courts, the other half being Clerkenwell. So these two courts, whose histories had represented two fundamentally different if parallel traditions under the umbrella of the magistracy, found themselves amalgamated at last. In theory, they should have formed one Bench, sharing out the workload and the courts between them. In practice, things did not work out like that.

Clerkenwell, which by this time had three stipendiary magistrates sitting all day in both courtrooms turn by turn, saw no reason to change its habits for a collection of non-professionals from Hampstead. The Hampstead Justices and their Clerks were equally resistant to having their autonomy disturbed by the presence of a stipendiary. There, for many years, the matter rested. As had long been the practice, complicated cases which might not be over in one day were sent to Clerkenwell, or sometimes Marylebone, because JPs are not normally expected to sit for more than one whole day at a time; and in all ways the Hampstead Justices continued as before, having absorbed or disposed of their new, inexperienced colleagues. By the 1970s the Bench numbered around 50. The Clerkenwell stipendiaries found it useful to have the lay Justices take their place on one of those days when some desirable function was happening elsewhere (Wimbledon and Ascot are traditionally mentioned). Thus the JPs, abetted by their Clerks, who liked them, gradually insinuated themselves into 'dirty old Clerkenwell'; but until about 1990, no stipendiary appeared regularly in Hampstead. When one did, the lay magistrates were not there on his day, so they never encountered him.

In these circumstances, it cannot be said that the supposed West Central Division ever formed one unit. Neither of these courthouses had a dining room, so there was no natural place for the stipendiaries and the lay Justices to meet and exchange views. The Hampstead Justices felt it was not their role to approach the full-time professional magistrates, beings much higher up the court pecking order than they were; and, with one or two honourable exceptions, the stipendiaries of the last three decades of the century did not seem to regard it as their job to liaise with the JPs, even though these were sitting on the same sort of cases as they did.

As a result, the nature of West Central justice from the point of view of the man or woman in the dock depended very much on which sort of Bench they faced, and they (or their solicitors) soon learned to try to avoid certain days in certain places. The lay Justices were said to be more sympathetic to shoplifters, for instance, but for motoring offences they tended to abide, more or less, by the suggested tariffs now set out by the Magistrates' Association. The stipendiaries had no regard for these tariffs and sometimes gave motorists derisory fines, but their penalties for criminal offences were often much more draconian. They were also, on occasions, more individualistic. In the 1980s the area around King's Cross Station, a few minutes' walk from the court, was much frequented by prostitutes, who would be brought in on charges of soliciting under the Street Offences Act. One stipendiary, who was apparently bent on reforming the Fallen in the best traditions of 100 years earlier, made a practice of giving these women suspended prison sentences – a new and favoured means of disposal in those years for certain offences, and particularly for first offenders, but not one ever intended to be applied to those unregenerately pursuing sex as a business. His rationale may have been that fining prostitutes simply leads to them entertaining extra customers to get the fines paid, something lay magistrates had already pointed out in the 1920s. However, the result of a suspended sentence was that the next time the woman appeared in court for a similar offence – as she almost invariably did – the Bench, often composed of lay Justices, was faced with an unenviable choice. They could follow the book and activate the suspended sentence by sending the woman to gaol, which they did not think appropriate and which would cause the prison authorities to make disparaging remarks about 'stupid JPs'. Or they could proceed to the usual fine as if the suspended sentence had never existed, which arguably brought the Law into disrepute and made it look as if one courtroom did not know what the other was doing – which was indeed the case! The matter was never resolved, but fortunately, towards the end of the 1980s, Parliament amended the law in such a way that imprisonment for soliciting became a thing of the past.

In recent years, with small courthouses such as Hampstead and Clerkenwell being closed down, and successive governments attempting to regulate more and more by statute the way penalties are applied, lay Justices have begun to feel that their days are numbered. The very qualities for which they have always been prized – common sense, local knowledge, flexibility, a moral sense untainted by the amorality of legalistic argument –seem to be undervalued in the drive to make them ever 'more professional'. Meanwhile, the future seems to lie with the actual professionals, the stipendiaries, recently renamed 'District Judges'. As I write (2001) there is an insistent suggestion that JPs should sit with a professional in the chair, a concept likely to negate the advantages of both kinds of magistrate and to please neither.

It is, however, salutary to realise that the 600-year-old tradition of the Justice of the Peace has been in crisis, with its end confidently predicted, several times before. When the first 'public offices' were set up in London at the end of the 18th century, many people must have heaved a sigh of relief at the thought that this was the first step towards getting rid of the unsatisfactory Middlesex Justices. However, they did not disappear. Equally, one might have supposed that the removal of so many of the Justices' traditional functions between 1842 and 1888 would have marginalised them to disappearance point, like the parish watchmen of old: at the time, their end was certainly predicted. However, they re-created themselves in a judicial capacity with greatly increased powers. In 1907, the progressive Hugh Gamon (*The London Police Court Today and Tomorrow*) believed lay magistrates to be 'out of harmony with modern requirements', yet the succeeding century saw all magistrates' powers actually extended, with lay Justices, by and large, setting the pace for reform.

The three Clerks from Clerkenwell, Stanley French, F T Giles and Derek Wainwright, having spent virtually all their working lives with stipendiaries, were all rather wary of JPs, doubting if they could be trusted – but these three able, experienced men had learned not necessarily to trust the stipendiaries either. At the end of World War II the JPs' reputation was at a low ebb; yet 20 years later, trimmed and re-launched, they were reincorporated fully into the metropolitan justice system.

I shall leave the last word to Sir Thomas Skyrme, the principal modern authority on the magistracy, whose large book on the subject has supplied much of the skeleton over which this present slim account has placed some local flesh: 'The lay Justices of the Peace were the kind of historical legacy that one would have expected to be the first to founder in the revolutionary flood of the post-war years. That they survived this crucial period was due to the ability of the system to adapt once more to a new situation, as it had done on so many occasions in the past.'

May that adaptability continue to flourish in the 21st century in ways we have not yet foreseen.

Babington, Anthony *A house in Bow Street* Barry Rose, Chichester 1999.

Baines, F E (ed.) *Records of the Manor, Parish and Borough of Hampstead* 1890.

Barnard, David 'The Hatton Garden Police Court'. *Graya* (the journal of Gray's Inn), No.82.

Barratt, Thomas J *The Annals of Hampstead* 1912.

Byrne, Richard *Prisons and Punishments of London* 1989.

Chapman, Cecil M *The poor man's Court of Justice: twenty-five years as a Metropolitan Magistrate* 1925

Dickens, Charles 'The Prisoners' Van' in *Sketches by Boz* collected and published 1836.

Dickens, Charles *Oliver Twist* 1838.

Dixon, Hepworth *The London Prisons* 1850 Facsimile edition, Garland Publishing 1985.

Emsley, Clive *Crime and Society in England 1750–1900* London 1996

English, Mary P *Victorian Values: the life and times of Dr Edwin Lankester* Biopress, Bristol 1990.

French, Stanley *Crime Every Day* Barry Rose, Chichester 1976.

Gamon, Hugh R P *The London Police Court Today and Tomorrow* 1907.

Gear, Gillian 'The Boys' Home Industrial School' *Camden History Review* 18 (1994) 1–5.

Giles F T *Open Court* 1964.

Grant, James *Sketches in London* 1838.

Green, David R 'Little Italy in Victorian London: Holborn's Italian Community' *Camden History Review* 15 (1988) 2–6.

Inwood, Stephen *A history of London* 1998.

Nevinson, Margaret Wynne *After life's fitful fever* 1926.

Paley, Ruth (ed.) *Justice in Eighteenth Century Hackney. the Justicing Notebook of Henry Norris and the Hackney Petty Sessions Book* London Record Society 1991.

Pike, E Royston *Human documents of the Victorian Golden Age* 1967.

Pike, E Royston *Human documents of the age of the Forsytes* 1969.

Reach, Angus B 'The Police Offices of London' *Illustrated London News* 22 May 1847.

Richardson, John *Hampstead One Thousand* 1985.

Rudé, George *Criminal and Victim: Crime and Society in Early Nineteenth Century England* Oxford 1985.

Skyrme, Sir Thomas *History of the Justice of the Peace* Barry Rose, Chichester 1994.

Thompson, F M L *Hampstead: Building a Borough 1650–1964* 1974.

Thursten, Gavin *The Clerkenwell Riots* 1937.

Tindall, Gillian *The Fields Beneath: the history of one London Village* 1977.

Wade, Christopher *Hampstead Past* 1989.

Wainwright, Derek *A Clerk's Tale* Barry Rose, Chichester 1998.

Who Was Who vols 1–4 (1897–1950).

The Magistrate 1923–1949 Magistrates' Association.

The Justice of the Peace 1837–1910 Butterworth.

Transactions of the Hampstead Antiquarian and Historical Society for the Year 1898

The Hampstead Express 1895.

Unpublished sources

'Oppé's Ledger': transcriptions of the Hampstead rate books and other notes compiled in the 1950s by E F Oppé of Holly Mount, Hampstead (courtesy of Camden Local Studies and Archives Centre).

The Development of the Law Court as a Building Type PhD thesis by Clare Susan Graham. Faculty of Architectural Studies, University of Sheffield (courtesy of Michael Pascoe).

In the London Metropolitan Archives:

For Chapter 2, Lists of Justices 1842–1894 MJP/L/15–30 (some years missing).

For Chapter 3, Hampstead Petty Sessions Minutes from 15.5.1827 to 15.10.1831 P 81/JNI/47.

For Chapter 4, Dinner Books 1835–1845 MJP/D/3-5.

For Chapter 5, Hampstead Petty Sessions Minutes from 30.4.1867 to 8.4.1868, PS/HAM/A1; from 1.7.68 to 15.12.1868, PS/HAM/A2; from 9.4.1873 to 12.6.1877, PS/HAM/A6; from 3.12.1879 to 14.4.1880, PS/HAM/A12; Registers from 14.1.1880 to 25.5.1883, PS/HAM/B1.

For Chapter 6, Lists of Justices 1876–1894 MJP/L/23-30; Meetings of Magistrates at Sessions and in Committees for 1888 MJP/L/45, 47, 48; Hampstead Petty Sessions Registers from Dec 1894 to Aug 1900 PS/HAM/B4; from May to Sep 1912 PS/HAM/B8; Minutes from Jun to Dec 1901 PS/HAM/A/14; from May to Dec 1912 PS/HAM/A/20.

For Chapter 7, Clerkenwell Petty Sessions Registers from Jan to Oct 1905 PS/CLE/A1/1; from Oct 1905 to Feb 1906 PS/CLE/A1/2; for Jul 1916 PS/CLE/A1/41; Minutes from Jan to Oct 1905 PS/CLE/B1/1 and 2; from Oct 1905 to Feb 1906 PS/CLE/B1/3; for Jul 1916 PS/CLE/B1/35.

For Chapter 8, Hampstead Petty Sessions Registers from 5.9.1917 to 17.12.1917 PS/HAM/BB/10, Minutes PS/HAM/A/25; Clerkenwell Petty Sessions Registers from Nov 1929 to May 1930 PS/CLE/A1/88, Minutes from Jan to Jun 1930 PS/CLE/B1/72.

Index